As We Gather to Pray

As We Gather to Pray
An Episcopal Guide to Worship

Edited by
Marilyn L. Haskel
Chair, Standing Commission
on Church Music
of the Episcopal Church

and
Clayton L. Morris
Liturgical Officer
of the Episcopal Church

The Church Hymnal Corporation
New York

As We Gather to Pray was made possible, in part, by the Episcopal Church Center and funding provided by the Adult Education and Leadership Development Office. This edition was assembled and edited by Marilyn L. Haskel and Clayton L. Morris.

5 4 3 2 1

The Church Hymnal Corporation
445 Fifth Avenue
New York, N.Y. 10016

Table of Contents

Introduction ix

ARTICLES

How Shall We Worship? 3
by Clayton L. Morris

Worship and the Ministry of the Baptized: on Reclaiming the Centrality of Baptism 7
by Fletcher Lowe

Who's in Charge Here? 15
by Ormonde Plater

The Development of Style in Worship 22
by Byron D. Stuhlman

The Development of Hymnody in the Anglican Church 27
by Thomas K. McCart

With What Words Shall We Pray? 43
by Jean Campbell

A Place of Good News: Liturgical Space and the Proclamation of the Gospel 50
by Charles Fulton and Juan Oliver

Creating Art for Worship 56
by Ralph Carskadden

The Role of the Arts in the Liturgical Assembly 61
by Marilyn L. Haskel

Preaching and Praying the Lectionary 65
by Joseph P. Russell

Jesus Wants to Dance!—In Church!!—With Us!!! 71
by Richard Fabian

Some Thoughts about Worship in Congregations Numbering Fewer than Fifty 78
by Clayton L. Morris

Dealing with Liturgy in Racially-Mixed Congregations 87
by Ernesto Medina

PLANNING STRATEGIES

How to Form a Parish Worship Committee 103
by Juan Oliver

How to Create a Worship Workshop in Three Sessions 106
by Joseph P. Russell

How to Review and Evaluate a Congregation's Worship Program 109
by Joseph Robinson

How to Plan Worship 117
by Juan Oliver

How to Introduce Full and Complete Use of Symbols 119
by Juan Oliver

How to Welcome Children in the Sunday Assembly 121
by Gretchen Wolff Pritchard

How to Design Service Leaflets Which Are Helpful to the Newcomer 128
by Marilyn L. Haskel

How to Compose and Perform Intercessions 132
by Ormonde Plater

How to Celebrate the Triduum 135
by Michael Merriman

How to Introduce Baptism by Immersion 137
by Clayton L. Morris

How to Build a Baptismal Font 139
by Clayton L. Morris

How to Use Incense 142
by Clayton L. Morris

Singing a *New* Song: Not Always Easy! 144
by Mark T. Engelhardt

How to Recruit Children and Adults for the Choir 147
by Judith Dodge

For Further Reading 152

About the Authors 157

Introduction

This series of articles provides suggestions for addressing the variety of details which attend liturgical planning. The primary organizing principle for the collection is the notion that at the core of Christian tradition are understandings and patterns of behavior which are instructive for the cultural circumstance the church faces today and which provide resources for current use. This book is not so much about new ways to conceive and execute Christian worship as it is about understanding and adapting the tradition of Christian worship for an emerging cultural circumstance.

The church is in a process of reformation. As it attempts to comprehend its relationship to a rapidly changing world—especially as congregations invite into membership people from an expanding variety of cultural expressions and experience—the liturgical planner is faced with an exploding range of liturgical expectations. Liturgical plans are drafted in new cultural situations in response to the needs and expectations of congregations with cultural norms new to the Episcopal Church.

This process of reformation began not long after the publication of the 1928 Book of Common Prayer as clergy began to realize that Cranmer's liturgical sensibility, which served to enculturate the Christian faith to a medieval English culture, failed to speak to the sensibilities which were emerging in twentieth-century American life and culture. The church continues to explore, as Cranmer did, the best ways to express the faith to the people and communities it serves in late twentieth-century American society.

Variety in liturgical expression is not just reflective of growing cultural diversity in the church. Congregations also vary and the extent to which they are engaged in explorations of the need for adaptation. The congregational habits which inform the perspectives of the articles and planning strategies which follow are varied culturally and are indicative of a particular community's place in its journey toward new ways of being the church. The reader should not assume that the suggestions presented here are wholly consistent. Rather, this is a collection of contributions from a wide variety of writers speaking to a variety of particular cultural circumstances.

It is hoped that these articles will stimulate thought in at least two arenas. They are intended as practical guides. Contained in these essays are valuable bits of information which will be of help to the liturgical planner in search of new ideas, approaches, and strategies. In addition, the variety in point of view and approach taken by the authors reminds the reader that the church is in the midst of transition to a new way of being the church. Perhaps the recognition that the church is "on its way" provides a sense of hope in a frequently painful process of inquiry.

Articles

How Shall We Worship?

by Clayton L. Morris

Apologists for Anglicanism in America have routinely boasted to potential newcomers that a primary advantage of the Episcopal Church is its uniform pattern of worship: *As an Episcopalian, you will feel at home wherever you go to church.* While this claim has never been demonstrable, it has prevailed as a description of worship for Episcopalians. In fact, Episcopalians have always worshiped in a wide variety of styles. From congregation to congregation, style has always been distinctive, and, currently, in areas of rich ethnic and cultural diversity, the Episcopal Church worships in a stunning variety of languages.

When the 1979 Book of Common Prayer was authorized, few people would have predicted the need for anything more forward-looking than the new liturgical forms it contained. But as happened shortly after the introduction of the 1928 Prayer Book, it was not long before deficiencies became apparent. As the new book found its way into the lives of congregations around the church, problems began to emerge. The patriarchal nature of the language, clericalism imbedded in the ordination rites, the monastic style of the daily offices, and the apparent redundancy of confirmation are examples of shortcomings which slowly conspired to curtail the longevity of the new book.

In recent years, the Episcopal Church has recognized that it is a multilingual, multicultural denomination. Partly because the ethnic identity of neighborhoods has changed over time, because immigrants from British colonies abroad have brought their enculturated Anglican heritage to the United States, and because the Episcopal Church has opened its doors to people beyond its traditional cultural borders, the church finds itself dealing with an ever-increasing diversity of language and culture. The image of the church's liturgy enshrined in the standard Book of Common Prayer and uniformly celebrated in every congregation around the country is being replaced by the more accurate picture of a diversity of liturgical style articulated in over a dozen languages.

The church is also realizing that many of its people gather for worship in very small communities. Statistics gathered from parochial reports, for example, indicate that almost a third of Episcopal congregations number less than fifty. There is a growing awareness that small congregations do not thrive on patterns of worship developed for larger communities.

For several decades, some Episcopalians have sought to deepen their experience of faith through the use of a variety of spiritual exercises: the Cursillo and charismatic movements are two examples. The influence of these movements on worshiping communities has broadened and deepened the range of liturgical expression in the church, and it challenges the church as a whole to reconsider questions of what is appropriate and inappropriate in Anglican liturgical expression.

As same-sex couples living in partnership discover the joys and challenges of expressing their identity in the context of their ecclesial lives, they want to have their faith communities recognize, bless, and celebrate their relationships. Beyond the obvious dynamics which emerge when a community seeks to actively embrace the lives of lesbian and gay sisters and brothers, the blessing of same-sex relationships puts the issues of blessing and relationship into a new context, raising questions about the nature of human relationship in such a way as to encourage the re-evaluation of the blessing of relationships in general.

And so, Episcopalians who have usually identified themselves as the American cousins of British Anglicans are now faced with the prospect of incorporating into their communities people from a dozen or so language groups and every conceivable economic and cultural circumstance. The church is actively incorporating Hispanic, Asian, African American, and Native American people into its liturgical communities. The church faces, as well, the need to reconsider the basic assumptions about its patterns of worship. Liturgy appropriate for a congregation of one-hundred-twenty people is fundamentally different from liturgy appropriate for a congregation of twenty. The church is called to recognize the presence of lesbian and gay Christians as members of its communities. The church, in short, is called to address issues of diversity and inclusivity in ways it wouldn't have imagined even a decade ago.

In the context of this epidemic of "growing pains," the church struggles to relate to the society it is called to serve and, at the same time, to maintain its Anglican identity. Clearly, this process of transformation—the awesome task of discovering how the church can gather all God's children around Christ's holy table—is a calling of the highest priority. But at the same time, it is essential that the community of prayer into which newcomers are invited continue to be Anglican in essence and identity.

When established patterns of congregational life are no longer able to respond to the ever-changing circumstance of world and community, there is a temptation to invent something new to bridge the gap. Before the framers of the 1979 Book of Common Prayer began in earnest to craft a new book from ancient liturgical resources, they considered the possibility of rethinking the church's use of the 1928 Prayer Book. Even in the 1960s, as plans for a new book were well under way, people interested in revitalizing the church's liturgy published reams of materials designed to *add* liveliness to the existing rite. Currently, one hears much about softening, editing, even abandoning

Prayer Book forms in order to bring life to the congregational assembly. Perhaps, if the church were free to adopt a new theology, a new ecclesiology, a totally new approach to being in the world, it would be the best course to start with a clean slate. But that freedom doesn't exist. As a catholic community, the church must understand the gospel as it has been received and rearticulate it in terms and forms which are accessible to the people the church is called to serve.

What, then, will a renewed Anglican liturgy be like? It will be biblical. Based in the teachings of Jesus, the church's renewed liturgy will continue to articulate and draw the worshiper into the life of faith which is our heritage. It will be traditional. The renewed liturgy will find new life in the context of the church's history. It will be Anglican, seeking—as Anglican liturgy always has—an expression comprehensible to the people it serves. It will be ordered, recognizing that gifts from the past are best kept alive for the future in a liturgical structure which is intentional, documented, and held in common. And this renewed liturgy will be forward-looking, recognizing that however much the church sees its identity in its historical and traditional roots, it must communicate its message in a rapidly changing world.

Some have argued that the 1979 Book of Common Prayer and *The Hymnal 1982* are all the resources the church needs as it approaches the new millennium. Certainly, these liturgical resources are among the best in print, but it is their unique qualities which render them obsolete. *The Hymnal 1982* assumed that the constituency of the Episcopal Church was basically middle class, English-speaking, and musically literate. In congregations where that profile is accurate, *The Hymnal* serves wonderfully. But congregations in the Episcopal Church are no longer limited to communities for whom that profile of privilege is descriptive. And thus, the church busily seeks a more diverse repertoire of liturgical music for congregational use.

The 1979 Book of Common Prayer reintroduced baptismal theology into the life of the church with a baptismal covenant and catechism which call the Christians to "love your neighbor as yourself" and to "respect the dignity of every human being," and a catechism which calls the church to "restore all people to unity with God and each other in Christ."

The church, looking toward the beginning of a new millennium, is struggling with what it means to make a place for *everyone* at the holy table. The church is struggling to recognize Christ in the faces of every human being and to find a way to celebrate the loveliness of the entirety of God's creation.

How shall we worship? We shall worship as we always have, by giving everything we have to the task of proclaiming the good news of Jesus to those around us. We will remain faithful to the heritage we are privileged to celebrate and rejoice in. And at the same time, we will reach out of our sisters and brothers whose lives and circumstances are sometimes radically different from ours. Thus, in our exploration of new ideas about worship, a new way of being the church will emerge, and that new way of being will be reflected in an authentically Anglican and orthodox Christian liturgy which is, at the same time, reflective of the new world into which the church is called to live, move, and minister.

Worship and the Ministry of the Baptized: on Reclaiming the Centrality of Baptism

by Fletcher Lowe

Baptism is the basic sacrament which gives identity to and undergirds all the Christian is and does. It is not only a single event but an all-pervasive and lifelong process. Over the centuries since Constantine, its power and significance for the Christian life have eroded, its theology has changed. The challenge before the church today, in the midst of a changing cultural milieu, is to reclaim and rediscover that power and that significance and recover that theology.

In the early days of the church, not only was a Christian "marked as Christ's own forever," but—because of that baptismal commitment—was marked by the existing culture as an outsider, subject to isolation, persecution, and, at times, death. To take on Christ was to risk one's life—*literally* to take up one's cross. This identification as a Christian came through baptism. The norm in that early church was adult baptism. In the Acts of the Apostles, for example, adults came to be baptized, affirming their belief in Jesus as Lord, the result of the teaching and preaching of witnesses to the risen Lord. Infrequently, there are scriptural and early church references to "households" being baptized. It is never clear, however, what "household" meant: Other relatives in that house? Older parents? Aunts and uncles? Slaves? Children? The only clear model that emerges from the early church is that of the baptism of committed adults.

The journey for those adults towards their baptism was then known as the catechumenate, a word which means "learning with the ear." The catechumens went through an extensive period (sometimes three years) of reflection and instruction focused on the life and death and resurrection of Jesus, the Messiah. Instruction included renunciation of the existing cultural world view and its values; exploration of the Christian world view and the values of the kingdom of God; and taking on that kingdom view by being incorporated into the body of Christ, the church, through baptism. The impact on their new life in Christ inevitably necessitated change and, for some, meant finding a new vocation and breaking off certain relationships, even those of their blood family.

The baptismal theology of the early church is reflected in the New Testament witness. As a person "took on Christ," she/he was incorporated into the body of Christ, the church (1 Corinthians 12:12ff); became reborn into the life of the kingdom of God (John 3:1ff); and died to self and rose to new life in Christ (Romans 6:1ff). This latter understanding became so important that baptisms were reserved for the Easter Vigil wherein the whole community, including the newly baptized, participated in the annual celebration of Christ's death and resurrection. At that time the candidate, completing the catechumenal process, threw off his/her old self, symbolized by the donning of a white baptismal garment and the taking of a Christian name. One's identity, therefore, was "sealed by the Holy Spirit in Baptism," as the new Christian was "marked as Christ's own forever." In light of this, baptism was seen as indissoluble, even in the case of those recanting amidst persecution. If a person renounced Christian belief under duress, the church, as it sought to reincorporate the repentant, looked back to the baptismal birth/rebirth analogy. It decided that, since the person had been reborn, shared spiritually in Christ's death and resurrection, and was a part of the body of Christ, the church, his/her baptism was indelible.

With the coming of Constantine (274–337), things began to change. The realm, with the Edict of Milan (313) became "Christian." Accordingly, a major theological shift took place based on a sociological reality; the result was wholesale baptism of adults, with none of the intensive instruction. The focus on baptism shifted from the extensive catechumenal process of the individual, adult candidate to spontaneous mass baptisms of entire tribes, even nations, by the decree of a local ruler. Then, with all of the adults initiated, infant baptism became prevalent, evolving into both a societal and an ecclesiastical norm. The baptismal register, for example, in many European villages was the town's only birth register. A new baptismal theology emerged with a focus on original sin and its consequence, eternal death. Baptism, therefore, became as much a theology of fear as a theology of celebration. The baptism of infants took on an urgency to assure that the child avoided spiritual damnation. This "fear" theology included a doctrine of "limbo," providing an in-between "place" for unbaptized children. The other aspects of baptismal theology—dying and rising with Christ, spiritual rebirth, and incorporation into the community of the baptized—diminished in practical importance.

As baptism became an expected social norm with little concern for preparation or nurture, the call to be a "real Christian" shifted from the baptized to those specifically called to the ordained or the monastic life. As Bishop Thomas Ray of Northern Michigan points out, "For the first four centuries the catechumenate was the structure through which people came into baptism. Since then, we have flip-flopped that over to holy orders where the same conditions exist: long preparation times (seminary education or its equivalent), new names (the Rev.), new garments (the stole), new vocations. The old catechumenate has been replaced by ordination!" Thus, the focus on the minor sacrament of holy orders supplanted the more basic sacrament of baptism as the expression of one's true Christian commitment, demoting baptism, elevating ordination.

The practical effects of this post-Constantinian shift—with its significant elevation of the status of ordination—severely flawed the theology of baptism, resulting in some far-reaching practical distortions in the life of the church and its relationship to the world of daily life. The two most profound are in the status of the ordained and the ministry of the non-ordained. As "holy Orders" had virtually replaced baptism as *the* sacrament defining "true believers," the role of the non-ordained became increasingly devalued. Ordination, as it evolved, was where the real action in the Christian community was located. Thus, traditionally—at least over the past fifteen centuries—the ordained have been afforded prerogatives and privileges far outreaching those of the laity, from their disproportionately large representation within the councils of the church to the "pedestal" mentality prevalent in many parishes. The clergy—to borrow from Paul's analogy of the body—have become greatly enlarged and oversized members of that body. Services of ordination, especially those for bishops, are far more elaborate, require far more planning and coordination and people than anything accompanying a baptism. And—irony of ironies—there is nothing in the entire service of ordination for bishop, priest, or deacon in the current Episcopal Prayer Book that even remotely acknowledges that the ordained has been baptized! The medium is the message. How we have disconnected ordination from its baptismal roots!

This "disconnect" became highlighted recently when the church addressed the ordination of women. The real issue underlying the ordination of women was less our theology of holy orders than a flawed theology of baptism. All the sacraments of the church flow from the primary river of baptism. It is to be expected that those who are baptized will seek, as occasion warrants, those other sacraments in their life in Christ. Eucharist, marriage, penance, healing—and Holy Orders—all come naturally out of the community of the baptized. But we have singled out ordination—through tradition (small "t"), ritual and process—as being so special that we want to be careful to keep it doctrinally "pure" (by whatever criterion we consider "pure" at any given time). For some time, that criterion has been heterosexual male, so much so that, in the confrontation over the ordination of women, rarely was the importance of baptism raised. What had traditionally been a minor sacrament, we have made a major issue by isolating it from the major sacrament in which it is rooted! After all, when viewed in the total context of baptism, holy orders is but a minor blip—one among many other honored vocations to which the baptized are called, including salesperson, carpenter, office manager, and executive.

From this exaggerated role of holy orders comes the second significant distortion that emerges from a flawed baptism theology—the role of the non-ordained. "Lay ministry" has evolved into what lay people can do to help the clergy do their job better in the life of the parish as institution. Terms like "mutual ministry" and "shared leadership" more often than not apply to the local parish as the place of "ministry." Less frequently do lay persons see their work in the world as "ministry." "That's what clergy do!" Thus, "the whole sense of ministry has been collapsed upon the ordained," Bishop Ray concludes. A sense of "vocation" in one's daily life and work has therefore suffered significantly and cries out for new life.

To recover baptism as the base of theology for the church, we must move back to our biblical and early church roots before the Constantinian distortions: away from the fear-driven societal norm of infant baptism and its corollary, the exalted role of the ordained (and the monastic) as "the true believers," and towards a deepened sense of the equal ministry of all the baptized in their daily life and work. This reclamation is of particular importance in the world in which we as the baptized find ourselves today.

So, in our day, how do we rediscover baptism? Let us quickly look at our recent history. In the 1950s as congregations within the Episcopal Church grew and flourished, there grew a false impression of masses of people finding Christianity anew after the devastation of World War II. Prophetic voices, however, questioned this apparent renewal under such pointed titles as *The Comfortable Pew*. The 1960s raised the stakes as Christians such as Martin Luther King, Jr. assumed the leadership in movements dealing with societal ills such as civil rights and the Vietnam War. In its concern to connect the gospel to the struggles of everyday life, the very church to which the people had flocked confronted the superficiality of the 1950s. In the 1970s, the Episcopal Church was engaged in its own internal and institutional changes: the revision of the Book of Common Prayer and the ordination of women, further challenging the church's life and membership. Through the 1980s and, now, into the 1990s these struggles within the community of the baptized have been overlaid by a cultural situation begun in the 1930s and 1940s which is redefining the church's role in society and the individual Christian's life in the world.

Christians in the West now live in a world that is increasingly secular and neutral—if not hostile—to the Christian faith. That world wants to accommodate some of our symbols and feasts (such as Christmas) for its commercial interests and, in so doing, sometimes trivializes them. The world often transfers a "7-Eleven" consumer mentality to the church, expecting the church and its clergy to provide services such as baptisms and marriages "on demand!" Further, it tries subtly to seduce the Christian to its ways, attempting to blend the secular world with that of the Christian (e.g., equating the faith once delivered to the saints with American civil religion).

It is in such a cultural situation that the individual Christian and the church need to find an identity anew. Two historical models can inform us: the Hebrews in their Babylonian exile and the early church in times of persecution. The Hebrews, in their sixth-century B.C. exile in Babylonia, found themselves in an alien environment where the existing culture was seductive. It had its enticements of material prosperity and other benefits available to the exiles as they accommodated themselves to the existing culture and its plethora of gods. It was in that environment, however, that the Hebrews consciously decided that they needed to retain their monotheism and its traditions, that the God of Abraham, Isaac, and Jacob alone was to be worshiped and followed. So they told the stories of their faith: about the Creator and creation and of his gift to humankind of dominion, about Adam and Eve and disobedience and its consequences. They heard the stories of their ancestors: of the Patriarchs, of Joseph and Moses, of the Judges and Ruth, of Samuel and Saul and David and Solomon, always punctuated by God's graceful promises and the people's stiff-necked responses. Through such storytelling they *remembered* who they were: Jews! They learned to answer their own question: "How can we sing the Lord's song in a new land?"; by singing the Lord's song in that new land!

Their experience bears some similarity to our own. We are not as aware, perhaps, as they were of being "in exile." After all, we have not been driven off our land and taken into another. But all around us are signs and symbols of a world whose values are increasingly different from those of our Christian faith, creating a sense of being exiles or "resident aliens," as two recent authors have defined us. We are in a new situation. Now, as Walter Breuggemann has said, "Baptism is what makes us exiles." No longer, therefore, can baptism be seen as that special norm for infants with its mixed societal and religious overtones. It takes on exilic dimensions if one is to live into its significance. It becomes the mark of our identity as called by Christ "not to be conformed to standards of this world, but to let God transform us inwardly by a complete change of our minds" (Romans 12:2).

It is at this very point that the experience of the early church is so helpful. It was through their baptism that those early Christians literally changed worlds, changed direction, changed focus. Conversion for them was a transformation to a new world view marked by the sign of the cross. As the baptized of today, that is our calling, too. Except in some specific situations around the world, we, as the baptized—especially in America—are not under persecution or the threat of death for our faith. But it becomes increasingly important that we, as the community of the baptized "in exile," find our identity in "being marked as Christ's own forever." In the midst of all the competing voices of this world beckoning for our attention and commitment, we are called to discern the voice of God in Christ. How relevant is the story of Adam and Eve! Like us, they were confronted with the voice of God and the voice of the world: the Christian's tension every day! And we need to know *who* we are and *whose* we are!

In such a situation, how do we remold a theology of baptism flawed by the passage of time? The most obvious need is to restore baptism to its rightful place at the center of the church's life and that of the individual Christian's. If, in fact, baptism is the sacramental act which declares one "to be marked as Christ's own forever," then the process of living into that identity becomes *the* primary responsibility of the Christian community.

Those who developed the 1979 Book of Common Prayer (BCP) had some prophetic insights into this. Contained within it is a twofold revolution. The first—which transformed the worship life of the church—is the eucharist as the central service on the Lord's day. But the far deeper and more subtle revolution is in holy baptism. It is like a tulip ready to flower; and principal evidence of its first blooms is in the primary placement of the baptismal liturgy. Being placed first in the sequence of sacramental liturgies, baptism sets the tone for the other sacraments including the eucharist, marriage, burial, and holy orders. It is also evidenced in other subtle ways: in the blessing at the end of the service of "A Thanksgiving for the Birth or Adoption of a Child" (BCP, page 445); in the preface to the Creed in the "The Burial of the Dead: Rite Two" (BCP, page 496); and in the Form Two confession in "The Reconciliation of a Penitent" (BCP, page 450). But the revolution is yet to be integrated into much of the liturgies of the Book of Common Prayer. For example, as mentioned earlier, nowhere in the ordination services of a deacon, priest, or bishop is there any mention of baptism or acknowledgment that the person was ever baptized! The pastoral offices aren't any better. And there is no reference to baptism in the daily office, either. Surely, if baptism is at the heart of the Christian life, it needs to be integral to all the services of this church. Such integration is a job waiting to be done.

Within the baptismal liturgy itself, heralding the revolution, is "The Baptismal Covenant." For the baptized, it is crucial in living into one's commitment to Christ. It frames our life in Christ. It is the job description of Christians, providing direction for the practical ways by which the baptized manifests Christ in their daily lives and work. Grounded inwardly in a belief in God as expressed in the ancient "Baptismal (Apostles') Creed," the covenant moves out in concentric circles from life within the body to ministry in the world; from the apostles' teaching and fellowship to striving for justice and peace among all people. There is no dichotomy here between the inward and outward journeys. The one presupposes the other. Because of its importance as a signpost for our life in Christ, the covenant needs to be photocopied from our BCPs and put on our refrigerators, desks, and bedside tables as a reminder of the call to which we continuously respond in life. The "Baptismal Covenant" can also serve creatively as a daily self-examination or weekly preparation before the eucharist.

Another subtle revolutionary element in the baptismal liturgy is the question, "Will you who witness these vows do all in your power to support these persons in their life in Christ?" What would a congregation look like if it saw these words, "the support of the baptized in their life in Christ," as its job description or mission statement? The work of the congregation on Sunday and throughout the week would be "to equip the saints for the work of ministry." Quality time would be spent in nurturing the faithful for their particular mission and ministry in the world. On Sundays education would involve, as John Westerhoff suggests, small groups reflecting on the past week and the week to come, with possible suggestions for the eucharist to follow. In such light, the eucharist becomes the weekly opportunity by which the baptized are renewed in heart and mind and spirit in their calling to live as Christians in their daily life and work.

Liturgically, members of the community would be commissioned periodically for their work and witness in the world, a welcomed balance to the commissioning of people supporting the institutional life of the congregation such as vestry and altar guild. For example, the Sixth Sunday of Easter, known as Rogation Sunday, could be reclaimed as an opportunity to publicly affirm the work of each lay person (not just farmers and fisherfolk), commissioning them in that ministry. Such commissioning could be repeated periodically as people undergo changes in their jobs, perhaps in each month with a fifth Sunday.

What this sense of baptism does is to proclaim that as the baptized, the Christian is fully commissioned as a Christian—fully ordained—and the role of the parish becomes the enabler of the ministries of the baptized in the world. A springboard to that recovery is provided by Raymond Brown, a Roman Catholic scholar, in his book, *The Churches the Apostles Left Behind.* "Holiness had been too emphatically associated with special forms of Roman Catholic life, such as religious vocation and the observance of vows. The unique status of holiness given by Baptism to all believers needs rather to be stressed." His insight is not limited to Roman Catholics. It is our need, too.

But this is revolutionary thinking in a church dominated by a Constantinian mind-set, which sees a hierarchial relationship between non-ordained and ordained, where it is the ministry of the non-ordained to assist the clergy in the workings of the institutional Church. Such a sense of "lay ministry" hardly jells with scripture! This revolution, therefore, will necessitate a redefinition of the relationship between the ordained, taking their place among the laity in doing the work of the Lord in the world, with special focus on "equipping the saints for the work of ministry." As the Rt. Rev. Theodore Eastman has written, "The sacrament of baptism is the ordination of the Christian to ministry. Baptism encompasses both the delegation of authority and the empowerment for mission. It is the process of ignition that propels each Christian into the world in his or her own way and time." Christians are, therefore, missionaries, people sent into the world to work and witness in daily life. Without this sense of mission, the church is merely a reflection of the culture's values. It joins with other social clubs in a world that looks for good works without the sense of Christ in its midst.

Such a calling may heighten the differentiation between the baptized and the world in which they live. This will inevitably involve tension when the values of this world and those of the kingdom conflict. Yet that is the struggle of the baptized who "comes to have the form of Christ" (Galatians 4:19). Christ himself as he referred to his own baptism, saw it in the context of struggle in the midst of this world. "I have a baptism to undergo, and what restraint I am under until it is over" (Luke 12:50). It becomes the "work" of the community of the baptized, therefore, to nurture and equip and empower the baptized for ministry in the world.

With such a reclaiming of the centrality of baptism, our baptismal theology, flawed as it has become, would be renewed in the life and witness of the community of the baptized. It would proclaim that through baptism we are "marked as Christ's own forever." Therein we have our identity as the people of God. That *identity* is crucial in the increasingly secular world in which we live. We need to know who we are and whose we are! It is in that *identity* that we are empowered to be Christ's people in the worldly world of our daily life. It is through our nurturing within the community of the baptized that we are equipped for the work of our ministry in that world. In such a reality, there are no second-class Christians, and the ordained vocations are understood as one vocation among the many available to the baptized. Such a shift would reveal that the Spirit binds us equally together.

As Bishop Ray has said, "Christ's ministry seen through you, Christ's ministry known in others, is now drawing us and processing us and converting and transforming our lives, twenty-four hours a day, open, exciting, venerable, confident, loving, forgiving. I wish it for you! I would wish it for me! God, in Jesus, offers it to you, and offers it to me. . . . Live it! Enjoy it! Celebrate it! Never neglect it, never discourage it and never give it away! It is a gift from Jesus through the mystery of Baptism. We are a chosen race, a royal priesthood, a holy nation, God's own people," that we may declare the wonderful deeds of him who has called us out of darkness into his marvelous light. And he calls us friends, brothers and sisters, to share his reconciled, serving, apostolic love, "for better or for worse, for richer for poorer, in sickness and in health," for life, and for life everlasting!

Who's in Charge Here?

by Ormonde Plater

When they gather, all the baptized respond to God's call to participate in worship. All praise God, all are nourished by the Word, all intercede for others, all offer the fruits of their lives, and all eat and drink the holy gifts. One person presides, enabling the assembly to worship. Others read scripture, lead song, proclaim the gospel, announce the topics of intercession, serve at the table, and give the bread and wine. Each person plays a role in an orderly and unified act of worship, and each contributes to the whole. This active participation of all persons is based on several principles:

- The baptized are one people, or *laos*, with many different ministries. The church is not divided into two classes called "clergy" and "laity." A distinction between these two has no basis in scripture or theology. It became part of church tradition only in the third and fourth centuries, in imitation of Roman social, political, and military structures.
- Leadership is a function of the Christian community. Although leadership resides in individuals, these persons stand for and act for the group. They arise within the community and, ideally, remain part of community life. They never exist apart or in isolation. Leaders are always associated with a particular group of Christians in a particular place.
- To exist, each Christian community must have leadership. A leader is a member of a team that gathers, forms, and supports the community. In this team there are different kinds of leaders, and there is a difference between a leader and a presider. Only one person presides.
- Persons lead in the Christian liturgy because they lead in the Christian community. Bishops preside in the liturgy of a diocese because they preside in the diocese. Presbyters preside in the liturgy of a community because they preside over the life of the community. Deacons function as servants of the church and heralds of the gospel because they lead Christian ministries of care. Those who read scripture and lead song show forth in the community the truths they proclaim in the liturgy.
- Bishops, presbyters, and deacons commit themselves to leadership for life, and the community receives them as a gift from God. This gift is not personal, causing some

inner change of character in the ordained person; it is communal, extending and adorning the speech of the gathered people.

- By the power of the Holy Spirit, the leadership of bishops, presbyters, and deacons has a sacramental quality. Each order stands for a different type of ministry common to all Christian people. Each order focuses a particular ministry in particular persons, for the good of all.
- Each role of leadership is distinct from the others. The various roles should not be confused with one another, and no role should usurp another role.
- All the leaders function in concert. Without competing for status or prominence, they represent the harmony and rhythm of God's creation renewed in Jesus Christ and made visible in the church.

Bishops

In ancient times the bishop was one who presided over the local church, taught the faith, and joined with other bishops. The Book of Common Prayer continues this tradition. The liturgy of ordination presents the bishop as primarily "called to guard the faith, unity, and discipline of the Church." The ordination prayer speaks of the bishop as a shepherd and high priest who serves, pardons, offers, and oversees.

The role of the bishop, however, is not static but dynamic, for the gospel requires constant reinterpretation of the world. During the first three centuries, bishops presided over a church the size of a parish in our own day. Several presbyters (equivalent to the modern vestry) assisted them in governance, and several deacons (the church staff) provided administrative support. Starting with the growth of church membership in the fourth century, bishops became the administrators of groups of parishes in cities or larger territories. Presbyters took their place as presiders in parishes, while the role of deacons in parishes gradually declined. In the middle ages, especially in northern Europe, bishops became remote and often princely figures, with little contact with ordinary Christians.

In our day we are seeking to bring bishops back into the life and liturgy of the local church. To do this in a way that touches the heart of a parish, we must change the nature of the bishop's annual visit. Instead of being seen primarily as an administrator of confirmation (which many prefer to locate in baptism), the bishop functions more importantly as the chief baptizer of the parish. Thus, at an annual visit the bishop not only presides and preaches in the eucharist but also blesses the water and anoints the newly baptized with chrism. (The parish presbyter may do the water baptism, assisted by a deacon.)

The bishop also presides at diocesan liturgies. These include diocesan conventions, gatherings of special groups, the liturgies of Holy Week, and ordinations of presbyters and deacons—all important occasions in the life of a diocese. Meetings of priests and deacons offer an opportunity for them and the bishop to renew their vows.

The bishop often spends Holy Week in the cathedral or other major churches of the diocese. On Maundy Thursday or earlier in the week, the bishop may preside at a "chrism mass," blessing the oil to be used at baptisms throughout the diocese. At some of these celebrations the deacons or priests take a small piece of the sacred bread, called *fragmentum*, and bring it home to their parish church; at the breaking of the bread they place it in the chalice. At parishes where the bishop cannot be present, the bread from the bishop's table helps to signify the unity of the diocese and the whole church.

It is an ancient custom for the bishop to preside in the liturgies of the sacred three days, from sunset on Maundy Thursday through Easter Day. Chief among these is the Great Vigil, when the bishop presides over baptisms and then celebrates the first eucharist of Easter with the newly baptized. The bishop has a continuing duty to preach to the new Christians, telling them about the mystery of the faith and enlightening them with the meaning of the sacraments.

The great sacrament of baptism stands above lesser sacramental rites, including ordination. The bishop's presidency in ordination, however, signifies the ordering of the people for mission. Ordination takes place through the laying on of hands with prayer; this act signifies admission into a ministerial relationship, with the grace to do the ministry. For a deacon, only the bishop lays on hands, since the deacon is received into the servanthood of the bishop. For a presbyter, the presbyters of the diocese join the bishop in laying on hands, since the presbyter is received into a collegial body of sacramental leaders. Similarly, a new bishop joins a collegial body of bishops, representing the catholicity of the church, and thus at least three (and often more) bishops lay on hands.

Presbyters or Priests

Similar changes have affected the order of presbyters or priests. Their two titles reflect a confusion in meaning and functions that continues to puzzle us. In the early church (as in scripture), a presbyter was an "elder" who was a member of a conciliar body. In the liturgy the presbyters sat in the presbytery with the bishop, the chief elder; the bishop was also the high priest, designating one who offers at an altar. While the high priest offered the gifts in the eucharistic prayer, the elders stood in silence. When presbyters became leaders of parishes and presiders at the parish liturgy, they acquired from the bishop the name of priest. By the late middle ages, priests had become almost exclusively those who sacrifice at an altar. Their connection with the Christian assembly seemed coincidental.

Today we prefer to emphasize presbyters or priests as those who preside in the Christian assembly, including its worship. As presbyters, they lead the baptismal and eucharistic life in parishes, join with other presbyters in a college, and share in the bishop's sacramental and pastoral oversight of the diocese. What the bishop is to the diocese, the parish presbyter is to the local church.

As priests, they have a symbolic function. Especially in a church in which the high priestly bishop must usually be someplace else, the parish priest expresses the royal priesthood of Christ that all enter at baptism. In liturgy, therefore, the presbyter or priest must clearly be both the strong, loving, and wise leader of the assembly and a person of deep and sincere prayer.

The presider thus sits in a prominent place, visible to all, as a calm and dignified person. The presider's functions are limited: greeting those present, praying in their name (especially the eucharistic prayer), preaching, and most of all sitting or standing quietly. Other functions we commonly think of as priestly, such as setting the altar, historically belong to other members of the assembly. By appearing as a quiet and peaceful person, the presider encourages unity and prayer in the assembly.

Some parishes (mainly large ones) have two or more priests. In many places retired or secularly employed priests regularly attend the liturgy and sometimes preside. These additional priests vest and assist as "concelebrants." The ancient tradition was for such persons to participate by gesture in the eucharistic prayer, and to assist in breaking the bread and administering communion. Normally, a Christian assembly has only one presider, and only one person presides at any liturgy.

In the eucharist the presider normally vests in alb, stole (hanging around the neck and straight down), and chasuble. The presider does the following:

- Sings or says the opening acclamation (and collect for purity).
- Sings or says the greeting and collect of the day.
- Blesses the deacon who is to proclaim the gospel.
- Preaches (although someone else may do this).
- Introduces the prayers of the people.
- Sings or says the prayer at the end of the intercessions.
- Pronounces absolution at the end of the confession of sin.
- Proclaims "The peace of the Lord be always with you."
- Proclaims the eucharistic prayer and lifts the bread at the concluding doxology.
- Breaks the bread.
- Sings or says the invitation to communion.
- Administers the bread (although someone else may do this).

- Leads the postcommunion prayer.
- Sings or says the blessing (although this may be omitted).

In the absence of deacons (and other priests), the presider also performs many of the functions of deacons.

Deacons

For centuries degraded as an "inferior" order and used mainly as a brief period of preparation for the priesthood, the diaconate is now alive and thriving in many places. Ancient deacons were the chief aides of their bishop and ministers of ecclesiastical state; they also were in charge of charitable functions for the church. The modern restoration of the diaconate, which began in the 1970s, reflects the contemporary concern for social care. Deacons are servants of the Lord who care for the sick, poor, and others in danger and need. In this role, they are sacraments or focal points of the servanthood of all the baptized. They are signs of service who uncover and explain signs of service.

Recently the connection between deacons and the gathered church has become strengthened. Deacons are again helpers and co-workers of the bishop, carrying out the great work of servanthood and revealing the *diakonia* of Christ. They also bring their work into the local assembly, by gathering and equipping Christian people for service in the world. As we now conceive of them, deacons are leaders of Christian care in society.

The role of deacons in the liturgy reflects their leadership of service in the church. They are the most active persons in the assembly. They move back and forth, keep time and order, give directions, prepare the table, serve the meal, and clean up. Their cluster of functions suggests both angels and table waiters. Angels deliver good news (from the Greek *evangel*), carry messages, and attend those in need. Table waiters make sure that the meal takes place with smoothness and enjoyment. Similarly, deacons in the liturgy proclaim the gospel, announce the topics of intercessory prayer, wait on table, and direct the ceremony.

A parish may comfortably use two deacons in its liturgy. They normally stand on either side of the presider and share in the functions of their order.

In the eucharist, deacons normally vest in alb and dalmatic. Their stole hangs from the left shoulder, either straight down or attached under the right arm. They do the following:

- Enter ahead of the presider. They carry the gospel book and place it on the altar.
- Proclaim the gospel. (They also sometimes preach.)
- Lead the prayers of the people.

- Invite the people to confess and lead the confession.
- Bring the vessels to the table and spread the cloth, receive the gifts, put the bread and wine into the vessels, and place them on the cloth.
- If incense is used, cense the assembly.
- During the eucharistic prayer, turn pages and lift the chalice at the concluding doxology.
- During the fraction, bring additional vessels to the altar and fill them, as needed.
- Hold the cup at the invitation to communion.
- Administer the wine (or bread).
- Consume the remaining bread and wine (helped by others) and cleanse or cover the vessels.
- Sing or say the dismissal.
- Throughout the liturgy, act as master of ceremonies.

Readers and Cantors

The leadership team of a congregation includes those who read scripture and lead singing. Because they are leaders, they should stand and even sit where the people can see and hear them.

In the early church, readers usually served for life, and their ministry was an office with its own dignity and importance, considered a "minor order." Readers could read well, and a deep reverence for scripture marked their lives; in many places they witnessed for their faith with martyrdom. By the middle ages, the office of reader had virtually disappeared, as subdeacons and those in "major orders" took over the reading of the epistle and other lessons.

Today we have restored the function of reader as separate from the lay reader who is licensed primarily to officiate at the daily office. Nevertheless, it is desirable to choose readers as officers of the church—persons with the gifts of reading, proclamation, and faith—train them in the skills of their vocation, and solemnly install them to permanent office.

The main function of the reader is to read the lessons preceding the gospel. When the psalm is not sung, the reader leads it. When a deacon is not present, the reader may also lead the prayers of the people. The best place for the readings is a lectern or ambo in clear view of the people.

In the early church, the cantor also exercised a dignified and important role, singing the psalm between the readings. The cantor often sang from a step (*gradus*) leading up to the ambo; thus the psalm was the gradual. Usually the people sang a simple refrain after each verse or group of verses.

Today the church has restored this ministry, and many musical settings have been published for the psalms (including a set of volumes by the Church Hymnal Corporation). In addition to the gradual, the modern cantor sings the alleluia or tract before the gospel (where they are used), the fraction anthem, and sometimes a psalm or canticle during communion. Two or more persons sometimes join in singing these. As part of the proclamation of scripture, the gradual psalm is sung from the lectern or ambo. The cantor may sing the other chants at the ambo or some other place.

In many places, the cantor also functions as song leader, conducting the congregation in other parts of the celebration. This role can be particularly helpful in a small congregation where there are limited musical resources.

Other Liturgical Leaders

Eucharistic ministers, acolytes, ushers, and others with important liturgical roles are also part of the leadership team. They exercise functions in the capacity of ministers who help the main leaders. They should have a gift for the particular ministry, and they should be faithful, committed members of the community.

Eucharistic ministers should feed the hungry and thirsty at the door, as at the altar. Their role as ministers of communion requires a license from the bishop for a period up to three years. The bishop also licenses some of them to administer the sacrament to the sick and others who could not be present. Their ministry is not simply a new service of worship at the beds and in the homes of absent parishioners; by extending the eucharist, they gather the absent among the present.

In the ancient church, acolytes assisted the deacons in distributing alms, visiting the sick and prisoners, and taking communion to the absent. Acolytes should be as eager to carry lights in the world as in procession in church.

Ushers too are descended from an ancient ministry, the office of doorkeeper. Ancient doorkeepers guarded the assembly against the intrusion of spies and magistrates. Modern doorkeepers are more likely to express the hospitality of Christ to those seeking shelter from violence and strife. They should reflect the maturity in faith of the community in which they serve.

The Development of Style in Worship

by Byron Stuhlman

The Historical Background

Style in worship—as it finds expression in vesture, architecture, and ceremonial—has often been a matter of contention in the life of the Episcopal Church. Because Episcopalians have generally understood their worship to be sacramental and incarnational, God's gracious approach to us in worship and our grateful response to God necessarily take on tangible, concrete form. The task of those who plan and lead worship is to find an appropriate style for this tangible form. This is one of the many ways that the gospel becomes enculturated in particular times, places, and societies. The principles which Thomas Cranmer set forth in 1549 (notice "Of Ceremonies" in the Book of Common Prayer) were these: " . . . we think it convenient *[i.e., fitting]* that every country should use such ceremonies, as they shall think best to the setting forth of God's honor and glory and to the reducing of the people to a most perfect and godly living, without error or superstition."

These are still appropriate criteria, though in a less authoritarian age we would speak of Christian formation rather than "reducing" people to godly living.

Cranmer realized that these matters were a cultural idiom in which the gospel was communicated. The tension in the style of Anglican worship goes back to this era as well: the Book of Common Prayer (BCP) 1549, concerned with stressing the continuity of Christian worship, continued the use of vesture and ceremonial customary in the Western church, with judicious pruning for theological reasons, and of the architectural design of churches, with adjustments in use (the movement of communicants into the choir during the offertory). The BCP 1552, on the other hand, articulated a break with Western tradition through rejection of eucharistic vestments and much of the ceremonial retained in 1549 and through a more radical architectural redisposition of the church. Although the 1559 usage was an attempted compromise, tensions arose between those who preferred the 1549 usages and those who wanted to move beyond even those of 1552. By the time of the restoration of the church in the seventeenth century, there was a consensus on the style of Anglican worship, which did not break down until the controversies aroused by the Oxford Movement. From the middle of the nineteenth century, "high church" Anglicans have often been characterized by uncritical adoption of contemporary Roman Catholic usages in these matters or by a somewhat archaeological restoration of 1549 Sarum usages; and "low church" Episcopalians have resisted this catholicizing trend, although gradually adopting many of its features. While these styles generated considerable controversy, the rubrics of the American BCP have always allowed considerable latitude in such matters, and an attempt to tighten up the rubrics by a ritual canon in the 1870s provided a short-lived and unsuccessful experiment.

The Present Situation

The liturgical movement and the ecumenical movement changed the frame of reference in which such issues were decided by the middle of the twentieth century. Currently, the debate no longer focuses on whether vesture, ceremonial, and architecture articulates affirmation of the standards of medieval Catholicism or its rejection. The criteria have returned to those that Cranmer had set out in 1549. Indeed, a consensus has been reached by churches of the Reformation as well as by Roman Catholics on the approach to style in worship. Differences of style are no longer important denominational badges.

The principal present criterion is whether worship communicates the gospel in an idiom appropriate to the culture of a particular worshiping community. In the decade of the 1960s, style in worship often reflected popular aspects of the culture, but as liturgical renewal matured, style in worship moved away from the more ephemeral trends of the era such as balloons, makeshift altars and vestments, and pop ceremonial gimmickry. The charismatic movement and other renewal movements had a greater impact on worship. While the majority of Episcopalians did not adopt the uplifted hands as the primary gesture of prayer, speak in tongues in public worship, or adopt the testimonial and the altar call, the affective warmth of the movement helped unfreeze "God's frozen people." As a result, many Episcopalians welcomed the opportunity to give voice to their petitions in the more flexible forms of intercession within the present services.

The current approach to vesture on the whole reflects a desire for what the Constitution on the Sacred Liturgy of the Second Vatican Council speaks of as "a noble simplicity." At present the white tunic known as the alb (often cut in the form of a cassock rather than put on over the head) has been widely accepted as the basic vestment of all those, both ordained and non-ordained, with special roles in the liturgy. Historically, a new white tunic was the garment which new Christians put on after their baptism. Such vesture gives expression to the fact that baptism (rather than the educational status which academic dress indicates) is the basic qualification for participation in the worship of the church. Beyond this, special vesture for the ordained as a sign of their leadership in the community may find expression simply through the use of the stole or, more extensively, through the use of distinctive overgarments (the chasuble for bishops and presbyters, and sometimes dalmatics for deacons). The integrity of the ministerial order of the church suggests that the ordained use vesture appropriate to their actual order: presbyters doing diaconal tasks in the absence of deacons should not be vested as deacons. It needs to be noted that copes are not vestments of a particular order: when appropriate, they may be worn on festive occasions by anyone from lay person to bishop, although contemporary preference for simplicity suggests that they may be used less frequently than in the past. While there is often a preference for simplicity in these vestments, styles and materials often legitimately reflect distinctive cultural traditions (as may be seen in the use of African fabrics and Native American styles). There is a degree of freedom to suit the style of vesture to the occasion—simpler vestments or no vestments for small and informal gatherings, fuller vestments for important or festive occasions and large gatherings.

With regard to ceremonial gesture, we have recently come to be more attentive to the message that our body language communicates, and to question whether it fits the text of our rites. For example, some basic gestures—hands open in prayer, hands outspread or laid on people and things to invoke God's blessing, hands outstretched in welcome and greeting, and the cross as the sign that Christ's death secures forgiveness and blessing and seals us in baptism—are incorporated as appropriate in the unfolding of prayers and rites, rather than being superimposed on the Prayer Book from other traditions with different emphases and structures. Beyond this, gesture and ceremonial movement are to a large extent culture-specific. Those who plan worship need to be sensitive to the codes of body-language within distinctive cultural traditions.

The architectural disposition of space for worship in recent decades has focused on ways to give adequate expression to the corporate nature of worship and to allow for the active participation of the entire congregation. We now try to resist the tendency of recent centuries to "showcase" either the preacher or the ordained leaders of worship, their assistants, and the choir. In theatrical terms, the thrust-stage has been found to work better for these purposes than either the proscenium arch or the theater in the round. Few congregations have inherited buildings designed for the explicitly corporate and participatory character of contemporary Christian worship, but most buildings can be adapted to provide a more appropriate setting by creating a certain flexibility of the space. [Ed. note: see "A Place of Good News: Liturgical Space and the Proclamation of the Gospel" page 50.]

The Important Issues

As the Episcopal Church increasingly reflects the cultural and ethnic diversity of American society, two issues remain before us: 1) How do we find appropriate idioms to articulate the gospel in the midst of such diversity? It is clear that the idiom of British culture from which our tradition springs is often inappropriate in Native American,

African American, Hispanic, and other contexts. In addition a multiethnic congregation suggests the need for a diversity of idioms. 2) How do we test the cultural idioms which we use (including the English one from which we spring) against the criterion of the gospel, to avoid the captivity of aspects of culture which contradict the gospel (in attitudes to women and homosexuals, in attitudes toward legitimation of violence, and on many other issues)? Cultures, like candidates for baptism, only become authentic bearers of the gospel through death and resurrection. The gospel challenges every culture to die to all which reduces God's people to cultural captivity in a world which is transitory and, in the process, to give birth to authentic signs of God's reign already present in our midst but still growing to fullness. When there is no discernible difference between the idiom of the surrounding culture and the idiom of the Christian church, the gospel has become captive to the world.

As our worship gives tangible form to the gospel, it needs to respond to the culture which it addresses. But if it does not transform the culture in the process, then it betrays Christ. The entire rainbow of the church—baby-boomers, Native Americans, whites, African Americans, Hispanics, Asians, feminists, gays, straights, conservatives, liberals, radicals—needs to hear the challenge of the gospel. The gospel may speak powerfully to the agenda of each of these groups, but it cannot become captive to any specific agenda. When Christ's arms were nailed to the cross, he embraced the entire world and offered it new life. The church of Christ is called to manifest a similar inclusivity and costly hospitality.

Factors to Consider in Planning Worship for a Particular Situation

It should be obvious at this point that there is no *one* style of Episcopal worship that can be uniformly applied in every situation. A wide variety of factors need to be taken into account in planning worship.

- *The nature of the congregation.* Is this worship for a small group or a large gathering? Are those who gather young, middle-aged, older, or mixed in age? Do they gather regularly as a worshiping community, or have they come together only for this particular occasion? Do they represent one dominant ethnic culture or many? The style of vesture and ceremonial and the use of space need to be appropriate to the group gathered for worship.
- *The nature of the occasion.* Is the service the regular Sunday gathering of the congregation? An ordinary weekday service? How does it relate to the church's calendar of feasts, fasts, and seasons? Is it a pastoral occasion such as a death or a marriage? Is it a special moment in the life of the congregation or the community? The style of worship needs to be appropriate to the nature of the occasion. Penitential and festive eucharists, for example, call for quite different styles.

- *The space used for worship.* We have inherited a wide variety of church buildings, and at times we worship in "borrowed" spaces not ordinarily used for worship. Services need to make the best use of the space available, and different spaces will call us to adapt style accordingly. It is inappropriate to try to use, without modification, the style of worship which is appropriate to a large cathedral in a small chapel, or to attempt to use the intimate and informal style suitable for a small gathering in buildings which are intended for large gatherings.
- *The resources and talents available.* Do those who gather for this service have particular talents and skills which can be put to use? Who reads well in public? What instrumental and vocal musical talent is available? Can artistic talents be put to use preparing the setting for the service in appropriate ways? Does the church in this service offer the best of its talent in the worship of God?
- *The gospel.* Worship is not merely a festive celebration of a particular occasion. It articulates the way in which the good news of the crucified and risen Christ addresses, confronts, and transforms us on the occasion. We need always to be attentive to the way that the cultural idiom as expressed in style bears true witness to the gospel or contradicts the gospel. Cultural idioms need to be baptized before they are used in worship. When this does not happen, the gospel is distorted or betrayed.

Issues of style are ultimately issues of how we express the gospel in a cultural idiom appropriate to a particular situation, and how we let the gospel challenge and transform the culture that uses that idiom. The challenge of resolving these issues is not easy, and it never ends. Christ bids us accept the challenge.

The Development of Hymnody in the Anglican Church

by Thomas K. McCart

Congregational song was not without controversy almost from its introduction into the newly reformed church in England. Although this essay is limited to the English church, the ideas and arguments expressed in England certainly had their counterparts in the American church. What will become clear in this essay is the remarkable similarity to current discussions regarding congregational music. By understanding more fully the development of congregational hymnody in the English church, perhaps the current discussions will be enlivened and produce forward looking proposals that would not have been forthcoming without such an understanding.

This essay is essentially an examination of the shift from metrical psalmody to hymnody as the dominant style of congregational song in the Church of England and, as a consequence, throughout the Anglican Communion. Given the necessary limitations, this essay will focus on several significant stages of hymnody's development. Beginning with a broad survey of the early development of congregational song in England, it will proceed with an overview of some of the secondary aspects of the shift from metrical psalms to hymns, the legal issue involved, and the resulting expansion of congregational song which embraced a diversity of texts and tunes now characteristic of Anglicanism.[1]

English Congregational Song, 1530–1760

> Yea, would God that our minstrels had none other thing to play upon, neither our carters and ploughmen other thing to whistle upon save psalms, hymns, and such godly songs as David is occupied withal! And if women . . . spinning at the wheels had none other songs to pass their time withal, . . . they should be better occupied than with *hey nony nony, hey troly loly,* and such like phantasies.[2]

[1]In this essay, I have retained the original spellings, language, and punctuation of the authors cited.
[2]Miles Coverdale, *Goostly psalmes and spirituall songes* (c. 1535), Preface.

The beginnings of vernacular English religious song can be dated as early as the mid-fourteenth century, when Latin office hymns and other liturgical texts began to be translated into English for private devotional use, a practice which continued into the sixteenth century. In England one of the earliest advocates of congregational song was Miles Coverdale. In 1535 or 1536 Coverdale published a collection entitled *Goostly psalmes and spirituall songes.* "Drawen out of the holy Scripture, for the comforte and consolacyon of soch as loue to reioyse in God and his words," Coverdale's work, like his English Bible, was intended to make the word of God more accessible to the English people.[3] The collection consisted primarily of Lutheran hymns translated into English and metrical psalms, i.e., prose psalms paraphrased into metrical form (see, for example, Hymn 377). The collection enjoyed some success until it was prohibited and burnt at St. Paul's Cross in 1546, due (almost certainly) to its Lutheran bias and Henry VIII's failure to form an alliance with the Lutheran princes. Although metrical psalmody was off to a less than spectacular start, it would be only a few short years before one psalter would dominate English church music: the work of Thomas Sternhold and John Hopkins.

The first edition of Sternhold's work, containing nineteen psalms in metre, was published in 1547, and a second posthumous edition of thirty-seven psalms, dedicated to Edward VI, was printed in 1549 (with seven metrical versions by John Hopkins in an appendix).

While Sternhold and Hopkins were producing their metrical versions of the psalms, Thomas Cranmer, Archbishop of Canterbury, was actively engaged in revising the liturgy of the English church. The subject of music occupied his thoughts as early as 1544. In an often-cited letter, Cranmer set forth his views concerning what type of congregational song the church should have: " . . . in mine opinion, the song that shall be made thereunto would not be full of notes, but, as near as may be, for every syllable a note; so that it may be sung distinctly and devoutly."[4] Interestingly, the two prayer books of Edward VI make no provision for congregational song. The reason why seems impossible to ascertain.

The accession of Mary halted all liturgical and musical reforms in the English church, including the completion of Sternhold and Hopkins's psalter. With the return of the exiles came the return of the English metrical psalms. From the outset their return was not without controversy. Challenges were raised concerning whether the provisions of the Act of Uniformity authorized such additions to the prescribed liturgy of the church. One challenge was made from the cathedral at Exeter, where the dean and chapter took every step possible to prevent congregational singing in the cathedral services.

---

[3]Ibid.

[4]Cranmer to Henry VIII, 7 October 1544.

Before the end of 1559, Elizabeth indicated her inclinations toward congregational music in this clause of the Injunctions of 1559:

> And that there be a modest distinct song, so used in all parts of the common prayers in the church, that the same may be as plainly understood, as if it were read without singing, and yet nevertheless, for the comforting of such that delight in music, it may be permitted that in the beginning, or in the end of common prayers, either at morning or evening, there may be sung an hymn, or such like song, to the praise of Almighty God, in the best sort of melody and music that may be conveniently devised, having respect that the sentence of the hymn may be understood and perceived.

It is important to note the spirit of compromise which this clause reflects. The more eager reformers believed that they had permission to sing metrical psalms, although with clear limitations. The more conservative reformers were allowed to continue to use the traditional chants, but also with clear stipulations.

The two positions reflective of this early period were ably expressed by John Northbrooke and John Case. Northbrooke, who like many of the more conservative reformers was troubled by anything overly ornate or tending toward Rome, wrote,

> First we must take heed that in music be not put the whole sum and effect of godliness and of the worshiping of God, which among the papists they do almost . . . think that they have fully worshiped when they have long and much sung and piped. . . . Fifthly, neither may that broken and quavering music be used wherewith the standers-by are so letted that they cannot understand the words, not though they would never so fain.[5]

Case, while supporting Northbrooke's position concerning what should be sung, allowed a more elaborate style of music to be used in worship. He wrote:

> . . . only herein we differ, that they would have no great exquisite art or cunning thereunto, neither the noise of dumbe instruments, to fil up the measure of the praises of God: & I alow of both. . . . The Psalmes may bee used in the church as the authour of them appointed: But the holy Ghost, the author of the Psalms, appointed and commanded them by the Prophet David, to be song, and to be song most cunningly, and to be song with diuerse artificiall instruments of Musick, and to bee song with sundry, seuerall, and most excellent notes & tunes.[6]

Both viewpoints continued to find expression in the following centuries. Northbrooke's opinion found eager support in parish churches throughout the realm where congregational song had to be simple and accessible if people were to participate, requirements ably met by Sternhold and Hopkins's psalter. Case's position was reflected in the cathedral tradition where medieval choral foundations continued to provide support for professional musicians to sing the praises of God, and that "most cunningly."

Over the course of the next century, the dominance of Sternhold and Hopkins

[5]John Northbrooke, *A treatise wherein dicing, dancing, etc. are reproved* (London, 1577), 113–14.
[6][John Case], *The Praise of Musicke* (Oxford, 1586), 136–37.

continued to increase and the tradition of singing metrical psalms (as opposed to hymns) continued to expand. Although new collections to satisfy this increasing use were published, none proved to be a serious challenge until the publication of Nicholas Brady and Nahum Tate's *A New Version of the Psalms of David* in 1696. In a subsequent printing, Tate and Brady included a supplement containing six hymns, including "While Shepherds watch'd their Flocks by Night." Although earlier collections of metrical psalms had contained hymns, it is with the publication of this supplement that a shift toward greater diversity in congregational song can be identified.

The church was slow to accept even the limited number of hymns made available in the *Supplement* of 1700 by Tate and Brady during the first three decades of the eighteenth century. The most significant change in the music of the church was brought about by the number of new tune books which were published. In addition to reviving older tunes, these new books introduced several tunes in a new style. These new tunes, treated often in a separate section of the book, were more florid in character and would, as they developed later in the century, become a source of concern in some segments of the church. Many of these tune books contained a small number of hymns in appendixes. They numbered from zero to eighteen and were drawn from a variety of sources, "While Shepherds watch'd their Flocks by Night" being about the only common choice.

Although opposition was readily forthcoming, the use of hymns in worship, as distinct from metrical psalms, became increasingly accepted during the eighteenth century. The work of Isaac Watts, a Congregationalist, proved to be one of two significant factors in the development of hymnody in the eighteenth century. In 1707 Watts published his first collection, *Hymns and Spiritual Songs*. Divided into three sections—Paraphrases, Hymns on Divine Subjects, and Hymns for the Lord's Supper—the work enjoyed enormous success. Watts's second collection, *The Psalms of David Imitated in the Language of the New Testament* (1719), brought to a conclusion what had been intimated in the first Tate and Brady publication. The stage was firmly set for the transition from metrical psalms to hymns.

It is difficult to comprehend fully the radical character of Watts's work. For almost a century and a half English worshipers had been Christian in their prayers, but their praises exhibited little or no indication of the New Covenant. This observation led two commentators to note that "[m]any an eminent believer, who joined in the public worship for fifty years, never sang the name of Jesus till he arrived in heaven."[7]

The second influence on hymnody in the early years of the eighteenth century—and for Anglicans of greater significance—was the work of John and Charles Wesley. Both Wesleys were well acquainted with the tradition of metrical psalmody and both may have

[7]The commentators were Bennett and Bogue. No other identification is given. Cited by J. Spencer Curwen, "Early Nonconformist Psalmody," *The British Quarterly Review* 71 (January 1880):86.

questioned its adequacy before their departure to Georgia in 1735. If they had not done so, their encounter with the hymn singing of the Moravians during the journey certainly demonstrated a different alternative to the metrical psalms of both the "Old Version" of Sternhold and Hopkins and the *New Version* of Tate and Brady.

In 1737 John Wesley published anonymously his *Collection of Psalms and Hymns*. The collection consisted of seventy hymns and included items drawn from Austin's *Devotion* (a Roman Catholic collection), George Herbert, Watts, Joseph Addison, and five translations from German by Wesley. The collection was probably used only a few times, since in August 1737 Wesley was charged, among other things, with "introducing into the church and service at the altar, compositions of Psalms and Hymns not inspected or authorized by any proper judicature."[8] Interestingly, while the grand jury responded to most of the charges, they did not respond to the charge of introducing hymns into the services of the church. What is most significant, however, is the diversity of the collection.

Returning to England the following year, Wesley published another collection with the same title, and a third collection commended for use in public worship was published in 1741.

In 1739 an abandoned foundery in Moorgate Fields was purchased. The "Foundery" became an important chapel in the Wesleyan movement, and hymn singing played an important role in its services. In 1742 Wesley published a collection of the tunes sung there. The variety of metres and the setting of each hymn to its own tune (only one tune being repeated) was a bold step away from the extremely limited metres of the metrical psalters and the number of tunes in the common repertoire.

Although Wesley had commended the 1741 collection for use in worship, conclusive evidence of its use in the services of the church is lacking. This lack of use may have been due to the fact that Wesley's followers preferred the simpler "Preaching Service" which consisted of two hymns, sermon, and prayer, even though Wesley urged the use of the daily offices of the Prayer Book. In fact, the rules which governed the societies included instructions for the sessions to begin and end with singing.

As early as 1746, however, it was evident that the singing of hymns would not remain within the class-meetings or private devotions. In that year *Hymns on the Great Festivals and Other Occasions* was published. As suggested in the title, the collection contained hymns appropriate for various occasions in the church year from Christmas to Trinity Sunday. Since the observance of these feasts was part of the Book of Common Prayer, it is probable that they were designed for use on those days in the parish services.

In 1753 John Wesley published anonymously the first distinctively Wesleyan collection, *Hymns and Spiritual Songs, Intended for the Use of Real Christians of All Denomi-*

---

[8]Ward and Heitzenrater, eds., *The Works of John Wesley*, 18:555.

nations. This collection consisted of selections of material written by John and Charles, drawn from three volumes of hymns published by them in 1739, 1740, and 1742, each with the title of *Hymns and Sacred Poems*. Although it contained only eighty-four hymns, the fact that it contained their hymns rather than the work of other authors set it apart from the earlier collections.

The people involved in the societies experienced two distinct types of singing. In the societies, the faithful sang the powerful hymnody of the Wesleys and other evangelical authors.[9] At the Sunday parish service, however, they sang the metrical psalms of either the "old" or *New* psalters. Such could not continue for long, and by 1757 the use of hymns had expanded beyond the meeting house to the established church. In a letter dated 1757, John Wesley wrote that the Eucharist was "enlivened by hymns suitable to the occasion."

The important 1780 *Collection of Hymns for the Use of the People called Methodists* brought to a suitable conclusion Wesley's desire to provide a hymnbook for his societies. This book, however, was more than a mere collection of appropriate materials. It was in its organization a "spiritual biography of the sort of person whom [Wesley] called . . . a real Christian." In the beginning sinners were exhorted to return to God and, if they persevered, they would know salvation and sing the hymns of "corporate life." For Wesley, hymns were "a means of raising or quickening the spirit of devotion; of confirming the believer's faith; of enlivening his hope; and of kindling and increasing his love to God and man." Like others in this period, Wesley desired to offer an alternative to the "formal drawl of the parish clerk, the screaming of boys who bawl out what they neither understand or feel."

With the growth of Methodism came an increasing hostility on the part of the established church toward such "enthusiasm." Urged to be faithful attenders of the local parish, members of the Methodist societies were often excluded due to the suspicions of clergy. This hostility was also extended toward Evangelicals. Commonly despised by bishops, those Evangelicals seeking ordination were often refused and, if successful, often found themselves unable to secure an appointment. One identifying badge was the use of hymns.

Throughout the eighteenth century, numerous proposals for the revitalization of parochial church music were suggested by advocates for reform. Charity choirs, itinerant singing-masters, various revisions of existing psalters as well as new versions, singing galleries, the publication of singing methods, the rise of village bands, all were designed to remedy the perceived defects of the performance and limitations of metrical psalmody.

The introduction of hymns into the liturgy was viewed by some to be yet another

[9]The term evangelical, when not capitalized, refers to the broad religious revival which occurred in the eighteenth century in England. When capitalized, it refers specifically to the revival within the established church.

means for restoring congregational song to its proper place. Those who favored the introduction of hymns, however, faced enormous difficulties. The temper of the age was one that distrusted extremes, viewed change (when rational opposition was wanting) as "popery," and deemed "enthusiasm" as an attack upon reason and common sense. Hannah More, the famous author, captured the mood of the century when she wrote,

> A cheerful knight of good estate, . . .
> He dreaded nought like alteration,
> Improvement still was innovation; . . .
> He thought 'twou'd shew a falling state,
> If STERNHOLD should give way to TATE.[10]

The Early Controversies, 1760–1810

By 1760 hymns were in wide use in Dissenting congregations and had made some modest inroads into the established church due primarily to the work of John and Charles Wesley and, to a lesser extent, that of George Whitefield and others. The majority of Anglican clergy, however, viewed the inclusion of hymns in the liturgy with dismay for several reasons. Most prominent was the still strong belief that hymns of human invention were inappropriate in the liturgy, a belief that had its origins in the Reformation's stress on the centrality of the Bible for the church. The clergy also cared little for Dissenters and viewed their hymns as a potential threat to Anglican theological integrity. The Methodists were viewed as fanatics, and their hymns were deemed to be colored with enthusiasm; both fanatics and enthusiasm were to be avoided. For these reasons the hymnody of the Dissenters and the Methodists failed to bring about a shift in attitude regarding hymns in the Church of England in the latter half of the eighteenth century.

As the use of hymns increased, arguments for and against their introduction into the liturgy of the church also increased. These arguments stemmed from a variety of concerns that overlapped and were repeated at various times throughout the period under consideration, often without elaboration or additional insight. In fact, some of the arguments continued to be expressed substantially in their original form well into the nineteenth century, and even a few were still being used in the opening decades of the twentieth century. Although there was a wide range of arguments used—some far more substantial than others—a few concerns dominated the discussion in the controversy.

---

[10] [Hannah More], *Florio: A Tale, For Fine Gentlemen and Fine Ladies* (London, 1786).

The Inadequacy of Metrical Psalms

The most often cited reason for the use of hymns was to supplement the metrical versions of the psalms. The perceived inadequacy of metrical psalms to meet the needs of the worshiping community was not new. Watts had demonstrated clearly that both metrical psalms and hymns could work together in singing the praises of God and that both were necessary in the life of the church, each fulfilling their appropriate role. Dissenting churches had embraced this expansion with little controversy. For the Church of England, however, the question was far more controversial.

The majority of advocates of hymnody preferred to take a deliberate and cautious approach to the introduction of hymns. The psalms of David were not to be excluded, but it was deemed advantageous to remove those portions of the psalms not applicable to the Christian state. Others were not as conservative.

David Simpson, for example, published his first collection in 1776. Simpson recognized the pastoral necessity for continuing to make available selections from the "old" and *New Version of the Psalms*. Simpson also recognized that metrical psalms alone were inadequate to meet the needs of the faithful. Hymns drawn from the riches of scripture (not the psalms alone) and hymns congruent with scripture (though not strict paraphrases) used in the praise of God could produce "more lasting and permanent Impressions in the Mind, than those which accompany any transient Form of Words that are uttered in the ordinary Method of religious Worship."[11] Evidence was sufficiently abundant in the New Testament, Simpson argued, to satisfy all that there were no restrictions in the use of hymns as well as psalms in the praise of God.

Despite this support, Simpson had certain concerns with regard to hymnody. Most important was the character and type of tune to be used. For him,

> Brisk, solemn, lively Tunes, [were] best adapted to awaken holy Affections. Avoid therefore such as are light, frothy, and fantastic; and let all the Congregation join together in one grand Chorus. Such Words, such Tunes, such Singing as leaves us dull, stupid, and languid, answer no valuable End whatever. They are neither pleasing to God, nor profitable to Man.[12]

Simpson's aversion to "light, frothy" tunes was probably an attack upon the increasing use of secular tunes adapted to sacred texts as well as his dislike of the "methodistical" tunes (e.g., hymn 57, *The Hymnal 1982*).

---

[11]Simpson, *A Collection of Psalms and Hymns*, 2nd ed. (Macclesfield, 1780), xi.
[12]Simpson, 1780, v.

An Enlivened Worship

A number of those who saw a need for supplementing metrical psalms with hymns also expressed the belief that the use of hymns would enhance the services of the church. For them the contrast between the vigor of the Methodist society meetings and the often noted dryness of the parish liturgy could not be ignored any longer. Hymns, in their opinion, would not only alleviate the deficiencies of metrical psalms, but would enliven the liturgy.

Although many Evangelicals embraced hymnody as a means of revitalizing parish worship, none, perhaps, did so with more enthusiasm than Thomas Haweis. In his collection of 1792, Haweis argued strongly for a hymnody which reflected the "power of vital Christianity."[13]

The use of hymns was also seen by many as a means of complementing the observance of the feast days appointed in the Book of Common Prayer. The lack of suitable portions of the psalms for these feasts was stated often as the reason for including hymns in the liturgy of the church.

Basil Woodd was, perhaps, the first to conceive the plan of compiling a hymnal that would be a companion to the Prayer Book. Published in 1794, his hymnal was a meticulous fulfillment of its long, expository title: *The Psalms of David, and other portions of the Sacred Scriptures, arranged according to the order of the Church of England, for every Sunday in the year; also for the Saints' Days, Holy Communion, and other services.* For every appointed day, Woodd provided a metrical psalm for the introit (as provided for in the rubrics of the 1549 Prayer Book). Hymns were selected to reflect the proper of the day; other hymns were chosen for use at communion, for baptism and other occasions, and a few for general use. The effect of this collection was significant, for it demonstrated that hymnody could reflect the character of the liturgy of the Church of England.

The desire to enliven the liturgy of the church through the introduction of hymns also brought forth concerns regarding the appropriateness of certain kinds of hymns and tunes. William Riley, for example, was among the first to note the dangers posed by the growing use of hymns, especially the music being used.[14] Of great concern to him was the type of music that was becoming increasingly popular, e.g., the tune "Helmsley." Riley charged the Methodists with full responsibility for this grievous development. Although objecting to a certain style of tune, i.e., tunes which had dotted rhythms, a broad vocal range, and repeated phrases, Riley gave qualified support to hymnody, yet

---

[13]T[homas] Haweis, *Carmina Christo; or, Hymns to the Saviour* (Bath, 1792), Preface.

[14]William Riley, *Parochial Music Corrected* (London, 1762).

preferred metrical psalms. Riley held that church music, in contrast to the "light and airy" tunes of the Methodists,

> ought to be grave, serious, noble and divine; to raise the Affections of the Soul, with the proper Passions of Devotion; *viz.* Joy, Reverence and Admiration; and not the rapturous Strains of unhallowed Love, which pollute the Soul, and fire it with a wanton Passion.

Riley concluded,

> Since Music then is capable of being made acceptable and well-pleasing to GOD, and an Help to Devotion, I hope the Established Church will never follow the Example of these frantic Enthusiasts, in *stripping the carnal Lover of his* MOVING *strains and* MELTING *Measures*; especially as there is such Variety of Compositions which are far more suitable to the all-pure Worship of Him, who will not accept of that which is devoted to his Enemy.[15]

The reference to Charles Wesley's verse is unmistakable:

Who on the part of God will rise,
    Innocent sound recover,
Fly on the prey, and take the prize,
    Plunder the carnal lover;
Strip him of every moving strain,
    Every melting measure,
Music in virtue's cause retain,
    Rescue the holy pleasure?

Doctrinal Concerns

Many who advocated hymns saw clearly the enormous possibilities for strengthening a congregation's understanding of the faith. Nonconformist hymn writers during the first half of the eighteenth century had utilized hymns as a means of reenforcing the themes of their sermons. The Wesleys valued hymnody's ability to teach the essentials of the Christian faith.

Many recognized the ability of hymns to communicate the Evangelical message even if there were differences regarding what that message was. Hymns were especially suitable for those who, because of limited education, had difficulty in grasping abstract theological concepts when expressed in written form or in reasoned sermons. The repeated use of simple expressions of basic doctrine in the poetry of hymns, in contrast, brought home the teachings given through other forms. It was perhaps inevitable that the didactic capacity of hymnody would become a point of controversy. "Why should the church use anything but scripture to teach the faith?" many asked, failing to see that the metrical psalms themselves were one step removed from scripture.

---

[15]Riley, 6, 10.

The concern over the dissemination of false doctrine through the use of hymns must have caused a number of clergy to pause momentarily as they considered whether or not to introduce hymns into their parish. The ability of hymnody to reenforce positively the teachings of the church must have also encouraged a number of clergy to support the use of hymns. The problem was to ensure that the hymns selected for use contained teaching that was fully in accordance with the formularies of the Church of England. Some believed that this was achievable; others held that the potential dangers outweighed any potential benefits.

Summary

The use of hymns, as evidenced in this limited survey (the examples could be easily multiplied), continued to gain ground as the century drew to a close, and increased significantly in the first two decades of the nineteenth century. Although the introduction of hymns was, at first, cautious, the evidence indicates that it was not restricted to any one locale or to any particular segment of the church. Such is also true for those who opposed this development.

There was an almost universal desire in the eighteenth century to improve congregational singing (and the character of worship in general), even though there was significant disagreement concerning the method for achieving such reform. For some, an improvement in the performance of metrical psalms was all that was needed. For some, metrical psalms were inadequate regardless of how well they were sung. Thus, many advocated the use of hymns to supplement the psalms. These hymns, it was argued, provided the worshiper with Christological themes. From there, it was a logical step to seek to provide texts which reflected the themes of the liturgical year. In both cases, these hymns often were introduced with the desire to enliven worship and to strengthen the teachings of the church.

Opposition to this development was at first focused on the Reformation's stress on the centrality of the word of God in worship. As this argument proved to be less than convincing to a number of hymnody's advocates, the focus shifted to additional arguments against this innovation, including the inappropriate character of the tunes utilized. Some abhorred the number of new tunes being introduced, believing that they prevented many from singing, since they were unfamiliar. Some held that the tunes composed by amateurs succeeded only in being grotesque rather than contributing positively to parochial worship. To these arguments, other concerns about the authorship of the texts (i.e., Dissenters and fanatics) were put forth: the taint of "enthusiasm"; the dangers of disseminating false doctrine; and, when all else failed, the fact that hymnody was innovative. As impassioned as they were, such arguments failed to stop the increasing use of hymns.

Many believed that hymns had no authoritative position within the church. How then could they be used? For those who attempted to support their use through New Testament passages, others offered differing interpretations of the same passages.

The question of authority began to emerge clearly in the 1790s and came to the fore in the second decade of the nineteenth century. This issue proved to be the key issue in the development of hymnody in the Church of England, and it is there that we must turn our attention.

The Question of Authority

At various times throughout the seventeenth, eighteenth, and nineteenth centuries, questions regarding the legal status of Sternhold and Hopkins (and, in the eighteenth and nineteenth centuries, of the *New Version*) were raised. Those who supported the use of metrical psalms in the liturgy of the English church held that the Injunctions of 1559 were intended to allow their use "in the beginning, or in the end of common prayer, either at morning or evening." They based this position upon a rather liberal interpretation of the phrase "an hymn, or such like song." The fact that the title of the 1562 edition of Sternhold and Hopkins included the phrase "alowed according to thordre appointed in the Queenes maiesties Iniunctions" supported such a claim. This position was strengthened in 1566 when the title was changed to read, "Newly set forth and allowed to be song in all Churches, of all the people together, before & after morning & euenyng prayer: as also before and after the Sermo[n]. . . . "

No one challenged the practice of congregational metrical singing. Some did question, however, whether Sternhold and Hopkins could claim the authority of any positive enactment for use in the services of the Church of England. Did the word "allowed" in the title mean "required," as asserted by some, or did it mean "permitted," as asserted by others? If Sternhold and Hopkins was required to be used in the liturgy, what authority had established that requirement? Parliament? Convocation? Crown? Was this the only version authorized for use or did the Injunctions grant permission to any metrical version of the Psalms? Moreover, the Injunctions made no reference to the use of metrical psalms or hymns within the liturgy, but only to the use of hymns "or such like song" "in the beginning, or in the end of common prayer." The title of the 1566 edition, however, had expanded their use to "before and after the Sermon." By what authority had this change been made?

The concern over the legal status of Sternhold and Hopkins (and, by extension, over any metrical version of the psalms) diminished during the seventeenth century as its popularity increased. By the end of the century, it had succeeded in establishing itself in the minds of the people as the only version authorized for use in the services of the church.

The question whether metrical psalms were authorized for use in the liturgy of the Church of England—and, if so, what version(s)—began to be asked with renewed vigor during the eighteenth century and continued to be asked well into the nineteenth century. As the number of different metrical versions of the psalms increased toward the end of the eighteenth century, the question of the legal status of metrical psalms became more prominent. Likewise, as the number of hymn collections multiplied and the use of hymns in the liturgy of the church increased toward the end of the eighteenth century, the question of their legal status began to be included in the debate over hymns. Arguments in the positive were countered with arguments in the negative, and the debate intensified from 1790 to 1820.

Cotterill v. Holy and Ward

Resolution to the question of the legal status of metrical psalms or hymns in the liturgy might have been long in coming if a case regarding the issue had not been brought before the Chancery Court of the diocese of York in 1820. The cause for the case was the publication of the eighth edition of Thomas Cotterill's *Selection of Hymns for Public and Private Use* (Sheffield, 1819) and its introduction at St. Paul's Church, Sheffield.

In the rather lengthy preface (sixteen pages) to the eighth edition of his collection, Cotterill responded to the allegation that the "Psalms only are *authorised*, and that the introduction of Hymns is *Innovation and Irregularity*." The idea that an authority existed for the use of metrical psalms and that none existed for the use of hymns, Cotterill argued, was a "gratuitous assumption, altogether unsupported by matter of fact." Space does not permit a detailed presentation of the case as it proceeded in the Chancery Court. What is important is the decision of the court.

On July 28, 1820, the judge rendered his decision. The court held that, strictly speaking, no legislative enactment enjoined the use of any metrical version of the psalms or any collection of metrical hymns in the liturgy of the Church of England. This did not mean, however, that those opposed to their use could successfully prosecute in the courts. The fact that several metrical versions had been permitted and used without being contested led the court to conclude that, as long as their use did not interfere with the proper order of the liturgy, they could not be excluded. The same applied to the use of hymns. In short, the court gave greater weight to "unquestioned usage," i.e., the fact that the church had used both metrical psalms and hymns for almost three hundred years, than to the official formularies of the church—the Thirty-Nine Articles and the Book of Common Prayer.

It is difficult to state with any certainty what immediate effect this decision of the court had on the development of hymnody in the Church of England. One possible effect was the removal of any opposition at St. Paul's. It is also clear that, in the years following this event, the number of collections of hymns available for parish used increased dramatically. Between 1821 and 1850, seventy-eight hymnals were published, and in the next ten years an additional forty-three collections appeared. In comparison to the number of collections available between 1760 and 1800, the increase can only be described as monumental.

Conclusion

Throughout the 1820s, a number of advocates of hymnody maintained "the propriety of metrical additions being made to our church singing beyond the authorized versions of the Book of Psalms."[16] Even so, a certain degree of hesitancy remained. J. Bull, for example, acknowledged that, while his collection of hymns "may be suitable for general use, are we authorized to adopt them . . .?"[17] Bull admitted that, in offering his work for use in the church, he was treading "on tender ground." Yet he firmly believed that the use of hymns was not forbidden.

The attitude expressed by Bull is an accurate reflection of the mood of the majority of worshipers towards the use of hymns in the liturgy. Opposition to their use based upon the question of authorization would continue for several decades. The central issue, however, had been decided in Cotterill v. Holy and Ward. The decision by the court that, while no legal support could be found for their use, the historical evidence indicated that metrical psalms had achieved a place in the liturgy nonetheless—and, by extension, hymns also. Moreover, since the court made it very clear that prosecuting this particular breach of the rubrics of the Book of Common Prayer and the Acts of Uniformity would not lead the court to "condemn in costs," it meant that no effective means for preventing the use of metrical psalms or hymns existed. Thus, one effect of this case was to open the floodgates for hymns to be introduced into the liturgy of the church. Another effect was to provide an option where none existed rubrically due to the vicissitudes of enforcement.

Clearly, the church was not yet of one mind regarding the inclusion of hymns in the liturgy. Nor would the church come near to being of one mind until after the publication of *Hymns Ancient and Modern* in 1861. In the intervening years, the controversy over the inclusion of hymns in the liturgy would undergo a transformation. From 1830 until the opening years of the twentieth century, the debate was not whether to sing hymns, but

[16]Pastor, "Sternhold's Psalms," *The Christian Observer*, 26 October 1826, pp. 600–601.
[17]J. Bull, *Devotional Hymns* (London, 1827), x.

what hymns to sing—a debate which continues to this day. In that debate the variety of texts and tunes expanded considerably, embracing most significantly the heritage of the Roman church (e.g., the translations of John Mason Neale).

The evidence presented in this study suggests that the Church of England was more flexible and innovative than has previously been assumed. The blatant disregard of the rubrics of the Book of Common Prayer and the Injunctions of 1559 with regard to the use of hymns within the liturgy of the church by a considerable number of clergy indicates that the needs of the congregation exceeded the legal demands for conformity to the established formularies of the church, and that the clergy willingly attempted to meet those needs rather than blindly obey the formularies. In short, the law was too narrow to meet the needs of the church. Since it was apparent to all that the law would not be changed, the law had to be disregarded. Thus, every parish was free to determine its own style of worship within the remaining strictures of the Book of Common Prayer.

As this essay has demonstrated, the character and style of Anglican congregational style developed over a significant period of history and did so with considerable controversy, coming eventually to embrace an eclectic congregational song. In the end, the demands of the people far outweighed the legal status of their use within the services of the church. Similarly, the type of text and tune used also reflected the diversity of the Church of England. To say that there is one particular type of tune or that there is a limited number of text sources available is far removed from the realities of this development. The inclusivity argued for by Elizabeth I in the early days of the emerging Church of England proved to be the basis for what we now deem to be Anglican hymnody—hymnody which can embrace equally metrical psalms, Watts's "When I survey the wondrous cross" and John Mason Neale's "Christ is made the sure foundation," hymnody which can sing with equal vigor the tunes "St. Anne" and Calvin Hampton's "St. Helena" (see Hymn 469, *The Hymnal 1982*).

While the American church avoided this controversy (almost entirely) through the adoption of an official hymnal at its founding convention in 1789, the larger questions continue to face us, and appropriately so. For can one ever argue that we, the baptized, have found every way to sing the praises of God?

Although much more detail could (and, perhaps, should) be given, the basic point seems to be unmistakable—that is, as the church continued to grow in the eighteenth century and the early decades of the nineteenth, it clearly was willing to embrace a considerable diversity of materials for use in worship. It was only in the latter half of the nineteenth century that a belief emerged which held that every parish (and I would emphasize the word *every*) should base its music upon the cathedral model. Historically, this was a move away from the on-going development of congregational song in the Church of England. I would argue that the time has come for every parish to reevaluate its approach to congregational song. The heritage that is ours indicates that in the most significant period of development the primary goal was to provide the congregation with the best music and texts that fitted most clearly the needs of the people, always keeping in mind the theological constraints of the formularies of the church, but without being necessarily bound by the fact that they did not allow for congregational song at all. The primary goal was not to have a uniform congregational song—one song which was forced to fit every situation without regard to the particularities and peculiarities of the parish. We would do well to return to that primary goal.

With What Words Shall We Pray?

by Jean Campbell

A number of years ago I was asked to address a diocesan gathering on the eucharist. In the process of preparing for the conference, I was asked by the planners to speak to issues of cultural diversity in liturgy, particularly liturgy in the Hispanic community. I responded that I did not have a background to address the issues involved. I *did* talk with one of my sisters (we are members of the Order of St. Helena) who is Hispanic. In an extended conversation, my sister in exasperation said, "I'm tired of praying in translation." For the first time, I had the means of describing the struggle that Anglicans have been engaged in since the time of the Reformation.

At the heart of the English reformation was the assumption that the prayer of the church must be in a language understood by the people of God. In the preface to the 1549 Book of Common Prayer, Cranmer sets forth a rationale for the use of vernacular language for the reading of scripture and the prayer of the church:

> . . . whereas St. Paul would have such language spoken to the people in the Church, as they might understand, and have profit by hearing the same, the service in the Church of England (these many years) hath been read in Latin to the people, which they understood not; so that they have heard with their ears only; and their hearts, spirit, and mind, have not been edified thereby. (Book of Common Prayer, page 866).

Prayer is spoken from the hearts of a community bound together in Christ, with Christ, and through Christ in the praise of God. Liturgical prayer not only appropriates the language of the tradition of the church in a language understood by the people, it also speaks from and to the heart, spirit, and mind of the people of faith.

The words we pray about God and to God in our corporate worship have been at the center of all liturgical revision throughout the Anglican Communion. Language both shapes our experiences and provides the means to articulate our relationship with God. It is not enough merely to translate the faithfulness of one generation to the language of another. Each community of prayer must find ways to speak of its own experience and faithfulness to God within the language of our lives. Each community needs to identify and claim the presence of the Spirit of the risen Christ incarnated in the particular as well as in the tradition of the community. As our experiences of God and the world change, so too will our language change.

Development of Supplemental Liturgical Materials

One facet of the search for language of common prayer has been the development of supplemental liturgical materials. In 1985, the General Convention instructed the Standing Liturgical Commission to develop "inclusive language" texts for morning and evening prayer and the eucharist. The request reflected several movements in the life of the church as well as in the context of American culture.

The 1979 Book of Common Prayer (BCP) was in several ways the first truly American prayer book. The experience and the language of twentieth-century Americans are reflected in this book. During the period in which the 1979 BCP was developed, American English experienced rapid changes in gender-related language. Masculine pronouns ceased being used to include both men and women. The 1979 BCP was attentive to the inclusion of women in the texts of the prayers. For instance, in the psalter, the masculine pronoun was changed in a number of places to the plural, e.g., "Happy is he" in Psalm 1 was rendered "Happy are they." The use of the words "man" and "men" to include both men and women is absent from the Rite Two liturgies. These were just the beginnings of a changing consciousness in the use of language in American society.

New questions were being raised on how we speak of God. Did the exclusive use of masculine pronouns contribute to an understanding of God as male or one who had characteristics usually associated with men and not women? How is our theology shaped by an exclusive use of masculine terms for God? Could God be spoken of in feminine terms as well as in masculine terms? If women, as well as men are made in the image of God, can female ways of being and doing provide a vehicle for expressing our experience of God?

By the 1980s, the role of women within the community of the baptized had been radically reordered with the ordination of women as bishops, priests, and deacons. Women became visible in a new way. This visibility heightened the awareness of the role of women of faith in the use of scripture designated for the lectionary readings, hymnody, and the calendar of saints.

During the triennium 1985–1988, the first draft rites for the offices and the eucharist were published as *Liturgical Texts for Evaluation* (1987). These texts were distributed to test sites for use and evaluation. In the initial phase of the project, there was a naive assumption that merely changing pronouns would suffice. This phase might be termed the use of non-sexist language. However, the lack of gender-specific pronouns or even gender-neutral prayers leaves those praying with a sense of distance from God. In the English language, pronouns function as a way of speaking of relationship. The lack of such pronouns tends to distance the sense of relationship and intimacy between the worshipers and God. Merely changing a few pronouns or deleting pronouns would not be sufficient to speak of the reality of God which encompasses both male and female.

New texts needed to be written which reflected the broader concern for the inclusion of women and the feminine. The texts were developed in light of the responses received and submitted to the General Convention for approval. The final draft of complete liturgies for the offices and the eucharist was published as *Prayer Book Studies 30: Supplemental Liturgical Texts* (1989) and authorized for experimental use. An extensive evaluation was conducted in which over eight thousand responses were received from congregations throughout the country. Particular attention was given to patterns of response as well as to individual responses. The texts were further revised and authorized as *Supplemental Liturgical Materials* (1991). These texts were approved for continuing use by the General Convention of 1994 and have been reissued—along with supporting educational and explanatory notes—by the Church Hymnal Corporation as *Supplemental Liturgical Materials* (1996).

During this period, several principles for the development of new texts were established. It was assumed that the structure of the offices and the eucharist must be retained. These structures are common throughout western Christendom, and any new rites should remain faithful to the familiar forms of Anglican worship. In Christian liturgy, the truth of the gospel which proclaims Jesus as the Son of God the Father and Lord is essential. The terms "Father," "Son," and "Lord" are retained as expressive of that truth. New metaphors and images for God should be grounded in scripture and the tradition of the church. Within any liturgy, no single prayer can encompass the totality of the faith of the church. However, the whole liturgy must have a comprehensive expression of that faith.

In the past decade, the texts as well as the questions being asked about language of public worship have evolved. The current texts seek to introduce feminine language as a way to expand our prayer. This approach can be reflected in some of the texts. Canticles from the book of Wisdom were included which speak of God in the feminine term of Wisdom (Canticles A and B). The feminine pronoun is used to speak of God personified in Wisdom. Eucharistic Prayer 2 echoes Isaiah 49, identifying God as a mother: " ... as a mother cares for her children, you would not forget us. ... " A feminine experience of sin is expressed in Eucharistic Prayer 1: " ... we violated your creation, abused one another, and rejected your love."

The use of these prayers has begun to raise new questions about the use of the feminine in our prayers as well as the inclusion of female language for God. We have begun to enter a process in which theological reflection as well as the experience of praying communities are seeking to expand our language of prayer. Recent developments in Trinitarian theology, the recovery of the use of female terms for God in the tradition of the church in works of mystics, liturgical texts such as the canticles from Wisdom, and other biblical resources have opened up new avenues for expanding our language of prayer. New texts need to be developed which will reflect this mode of expansive language in the prayer of the church.

The Process of Using the Supplemental Liturgical Materials

Prayer texts can only be evaluated by their use within praying communities. There is a difference between praying and reading a liturgical text. Supplemental liturgical materials are draft texts intended to be preliminary explorations for the development of future materials for Prayer Book revision. In order to provide for the development of texts, a three-step process has been established. The three steps necessary are preparation and education, use, and evaluation.

Education and Preparation

All liturgy is based upon a set of agreed-upon assumptions. Whenever those assumptions are altered, there is the possibility of reactions which can range from confusion to anger. Introducing new liturgical texts without careful preparation is pastorally insensitive and pastorally irresponsible. Use of these prayers in any community demands a pastoral catechesis of the community. Pastoral catechesis includes time for exploring issues raised by the use of these texts and reflecting upon the prayers before they are used in the context of worship. The educational materials contained in the reissued edition of *Supplemental Liturgical Materials* (1996) provide opportunity for members to reflect on the nature of our gathering for prayer and for exploring individual texts. Another way to begin to introduce new texts is to use them with small groups who can study the texts before they are used and begin to obtain some familiarity with them before they are used as a principal service on Sunday.

Designing liturgies using supplemental liturgical texts will require careful and thorough planning. Decisions will have to be made as to what texts are to be used. There needs to be a conscious decision to use the texts long enough for worshipers to gain some familiarity with the prayers. Texts need to be used for a sufficient period of time to determine which prayers engage, nourish, and sustain us in our relationship to God. Only after using the texts for a significant period of time can people begin to answer whether they sustain and nourish the prayer of the community as well as inform and nurture their own personal prayer.

Decisions need to be made on what materials need to be in the hands of the congregation. For some this will mean a simple insertion of a text in a bulletin; for those using the complete liturgies it will mean the development of a service booklet. A CD-ROM version of the *Supplemental Liturgical Materials* (1996) is now available from the Church Hymnal Corporation.

Those who preside over the prayer of the community have a particular responsibility to study and reflect upon the prayers. One needs to read and to meditate upon these texts prior to voicing them as the prayer of the whole community.

Use of Supplemental Liturgical Materials

Supplemental Liturgical Materials may only be used with the permission of the diocesan bishop or other ecclesiastical authority. This authorization has a twofold purpose: first, it recognizes and affirms the bishop as the source and unity of the prayer of the church, and second, it provides a point of dialogue for the ongoing experience and development of the rites. Liturgical development needs to be done within the unity of the whole church where there is a framework for theological reflection and dialogue.

The supplemental liturgical texts are intended to be resources for the life of the church. The texts may be used in two very different ways. First, any of the texts may be used in conjunction with the Rite Two liturgies of the 1979 BCP. For instance, the canticles may be used in the context of a Rite Two morning or evening prayer or as an alternative to the Gloria in the eucharist; or one of the supplemental eucharist prayers may be used within a Rite Two eucharist. The second option is to develop an entire liturgy using the supplemental texts. The entire eucharistic liturgy can be designed with only the collect of the day from the BCP being added. Either of these options can be authorized for a principal Sunday morning service.

"An Order for Celebrating the Holy Eucharist," found on page 400 of the BCP, may also be used in conjunction with the "Forms for the Eucharistic Prayer" in the supplemental materials. This option provides a means whereby groups who wish to begin to write their own prayers may use them in worship, except at the principal service on Sunday. New texts might include collects, forms for the prayers of the people, post-communion prayers, canticles, etc. The "Forms for the Eucharistic Prayer" provide a framework of the traditional elements of a eucharistic prayer which can be used as a basis for new expressions of thanksgiving and praise.

Congregations who may not have the gifts to compose extensive texts might explore a few options which are flexible under the rubrics of the BCP. The option to evolve prayers of the people within a congregation has been in place since the advent of the 1979 BCP. General areas of concern are outlined on page 383 of the BCP, but the prayer itself may be written within the local congregation. Only after some fifteen years have a few congregations begun to exercise this option. Gathering together members of the congregation and working with them in a ministry of intercessory prayer and providing some skills in writing texts can be a creative way of engaging the life of the whole community in prayer. [Ed. note: see "How to Compose and Perform Intercessions" by Ormonde Plater elsewhere in this book.] It is recommended that a common congregational response be used on a consistent basis; then the text can easily change from Sunday to Sunday. Further suggestions on the prayers of the people are found in the supplemental liturgical materials. The collect at the conclusion of the prayers of the people is not a prescribed collect. Those congregations who are in the process of developing prayers may use this opportunity to explore new options.

Music is a major consideration in designing any liturgy. Hymn texts also offer a rich diversity in ways of speaking of God. There is a body of hymnody in *The Hymnal 1982* which already expands our language for God and is consistent with the supplemental texts in regard to references to human beings. For instance hymn #371 praises the Holy Trinity in non-gender-related language. Often metrical settings of psalms and canticles reflect modern linguistic changes and are appropriate when designing liturgies using the supplemental texts. Music is also available for Eucharistic Prayers 1 and 2 in the *Supplemental Liturgical Materials.*

Women are increasingly visible in our worshiping communities, a change that began with the inclusion of women in ordained ministry and continued with an increase in women as lectors, intercessors, and acolytes. However, there still are subtle ways in which women continue to remain invisible. The choices of lectionary readings in the Episcopal eucharistic lectionary has often ignored or diminished the place of women in salvation history. *The Revised Common Lectionary* was authorized for trial use by the 71st General Convention. This lectionary seeks to expand the scripture appointed for the Sunday eucharist to include passages which reflect the faithful witness of women. Congregations using the supplemental materials might explore the use of this lectionary.

The context in which the supplemental liturgical materials are used will shape the experience of these prayers. Non-verbal language—the language of gesture, movement, sign—will always override the text of the prayer. Therefore, care needs to be taken with the setting of these prayers. Liturgical ministry should reflect the fullness of the worshiping community.

Evaluation

All liturgical texts are rich in what they say about God but also what they say about ourselves in relationship with God. This is at the heart of any theological reflection upon the experience of liturgical prayer. Who does the text say God is, who does it say we are, and, most importantly, what does this mean for us? These questions form the basis upon which the community can explore whether these prayers speak in the hearts, minds, and spirit of the community of faith.

Included as an appendix to *Supplemental Liturgical Materials* (1996) is a form for evaluation. This instrument is intended to be utilized after a sustained period of use of the materials. It provides a consistent means of evaluating these texts throughout the church. Completed evaluation forms should be sent to the Office for Liturgy and Music at the Episcopal Church Center, 815 Second Avenue, New York, NY 10017.

New prayers which have been used and reflected upon within a congregation should also be sent to the Standing Liturgical Commission at the Episcopal Church Center. Only as materials are collected and evaluated will the church begin to have prayers which may in the future contribute to the prayer of the church.

Conclusion

The task is not merely to translate but to find the voice of prayer in the hearts, spirit, and mind of the people praying. The process of enriching our prayer is by nature an extended process requiring use, evaluation, and theological reflection. As the process unfolds, new questions are raised and new avenues of expression are disclosed. As the church looks toward the future, the possibilities of revising the Book of Common Prayer have already been raised at the 1994 General Convention, which instructed the Standing Liturgical Commission to provide a rationale and a pastorally-sensitive plan for such a revision. As theologians and the community of the baptized grapple with questions such as the naming of the Trinity, old truths are reclaimed, and we discover a fullness of the expression of our God.

A Place of Good News: Liturgical Space and the Proclamation of the Gospel

by Charles Fulton and Juan Oliver

The Christian people proclaim the good news of Christ in our gathering week by week for worship. We assemble to enact a felt vision of God's reign of justice and peace, radically including all creation in a celebration of God's ongoing great deeds: the creation of the world and its healing through the life, ministry, death, and resurrection of Jesus and his presence in the world through the members of his Body. Through symbolic actions made up of words, music, vesture, movement, and environment, we rehearse this reign among us, so that we may proclaim to the world in our daily lives "that which we have seen and heard . . . the Word of life . . . " (I John 1:1). One of the most important elements through which we form a felt sense of God's reign is our gathering place.

Much writing about liturgy treats the place of the liturgy as a mere background. However, precisely because it works largely at an unconscious level, the place where we gather for worship has enormous power to form (and deform) our religious experience.

Thinking About Buildings

A building is a form of language in its own right: it says, "This is our place, these are the kinds of things we do here." Buildings determine the range of our body language, even while most of us, including our clergy, are often utterly unaware of what our bodies are saying.

A building also tells us, its dwellers, who we are: the people who gather regularly at God's table. Above all, a building is "our place." For this reason, a building has great influence on a community's understanding of itself and its mission. In our buildings, our people teach us from the lectern, ambo, or pulpit; they birth us as members at the font; they feed us at the table; and often they lovingly deposit our bodies and ashes in the garden. It is no coincidence that we give our name as a people, *The Church,* to the building where we gather. A church building is above all the place of a people: a community with a diversity of roles and charisms, sharing a single space.

However, due to the accidents of history and the issues that have formed us as a denomination, our buildings often fail colossally to do this.

We have thought of religious buildings as inert backdrops for the recitation of texts; or we have filled our spaces with Victorian clutter; or we have only thought of what buildings mean to individuals at solitary prayer. We have thought about buildings as the containers of passive bodies, so much so that we usually tolerate a person daydreaming, going to sleep, or leaving, but often do not encourage active participation.

Our buildings are often spaces divided into two rooms, generating a divided people: a clerical or clericalized, active part of the church, moving about the sanctuary, and a lay, passive church sitting in the nave. Often the communion rail marks the boundary between these two rooms.

The two rooms have been understood as hierarchically ordered, (the sanctuary is heaven; the nave, earth) or therapeutically arranged (the professional caregivers in the sanctuary, their charges in the nave) or even in a commercial mode (the purveyors of grace inhabit the sanctuary, the consumers, the nave).

Behind these assumptions lies our historical investment in individual conscience and individual freedom, our seventeenth-century Anglican defense of the Crown and the exaltedness of the eucharist and the ordained priesthood—all responses to Puritan positions.

We also tend to think of religious experience as individual: " . . . the building works when I am in it alone," we often hear a parishioner say. In our valuing individual, private religious experience, we have ended up with an architectural model which prevents people from moving around or relating to others, and, while safeguarding a high degree of privacy, we have made each other self-conscious and anonymous, encouraging a private, almost catatonic, participation.

But God doesn't want us to shut down. The liturgy assumes that the assembly of the Christian people is the central symbolic element in worship. Because, and insofar as, we are the body of Christ, our liturgical actions can manifest the presence of God's reign of justice and peace among us today.

New Book, Old Dance

The 1979 Book of Common Prayer combines the classical structure of the liturgy with an understanding of the people of God as the central expression of the mystery of Christ. The sacraments of Christian initiation (baptism, anointing, eucharist) have been once again given pride of place among the ritual actions of the Christian people, and this has given rise to a new awareness of the ministry of all Christians in liturgy and everyday life.

But just as we have developed new texts for worship, hoping to reform the church to a more authentic expression as the people of God in Christ, we can acknowledge also the role of everything else that takes place in worship besides the text, attending especially to the formative role of the building.

Our buildings continue both to express and to create an understanding of the church more typical of the 1928 Book of Common Prayer and the morning prayer tradition. We have inherited buildings which present a nineteenth-century sense of the sacred as something distant, dark, and mysterious, encouraging silence, introspection and awe. As a result, many parishes and missions celebrate the eucharist of 1979 with the choreography and architecture of 1928.

But our culture has moved on, and nowadays we find the sacred not mainly in these Victorian ways but, above all, in nature, the creative process, and the self. Thus, buildings which present the congregation's valuing of these three manifestations of the sacred—in the created order, in the arts, and in the persons involved—will communicate a more contemporary feeling of the sacred than will "traditional" Victorian buildings.

Additionally, these Victorian spaces assumed an individualistic piety on the part of the participants, embodying a romantic yearning for a mythic medieval sense of awe and order; when, in fact, medieval church buildings were likely bustling places, packed with a mass of humanity chatting, selling and buying, saying prayers before shrines, lighting candles, and venerating relics.

In order to engage a contemporary sense of the sacred, we might design a worship place based on what is needed by the whole community for its liturgical and fellowship practice, and not based on individual lay or clerical needs and preferences. Such a building might exhibit the following traits:

- *Creates flexibility:* Different liturgical situations can profit from taking place in different spatial arrangements. The Christian people might not gather for a funeral the same way they gather for a Sunday eucharist; or daily evening prayer might take place in a spatial arrangement different from that of the eucharist.
- *Establishes a single room:* The assembly, including all its liturgical ministers, should gather in a single space at any one time. It may indeed gather successively in different places, depending on the nature of the rite, but it gathers as *one* people, served by a variety of gifts and ministries. The seventeenth-century practice of bringing communicants into the chancel to stand around the table for eucharist is a historical example of this sense of the assembly acting as one.

  To test the unity of their space, Christians might ask several questions: To whom does the space belong? Whose is it? Who has access to which parts? Why? Are there divisions in the space? Between clergy and laity? Between baptized and unbaptized? What are the theological implications of these divisions? What kind of power relationships are generated and sustained by them?

- *Encourages full capacity:* The worship space is designed to make sense when full of participants, not as a "shrine" designed for individual veneration. A good liturgical space might contain such places for individual prayer or meditation, but these are secondary to the main purpose of the building: to gather the Christian people and help them to worship as a body.

- *Reveals an active assembly:* A good liturgical space reveals the assembly as the doers of worship, led by an officiant or priestly presider and other liturgical ministers. It does not treat the assembly as passive spectators.

- *Enables symbolic actions:* Symbolic actions must be allowed without abbreviation. The space *encourages* the congregation to listen to the scriptures proclaimed and to share their meaning; to wash people and anoint; to pray for church and world; to give thanks over a ritual meal and share in eating bread and drinking wine; to gather for fellowship. In facilitating these ritual actions, the building encourages the assembly to engage symbolic elements such as ashes, water, oil, bread, and wine; symbolic objects such as ambo, scripture volumes, musical instruments, table, and font; and honorifics such as candles, incense, and flowers as appropriate to the liturgical action.

- *Encourages engaged participation:* The building aids its dwellers in taking part in the ritual action. However, this does not mean that every member of the assembly must do everything. The assembly is made up of different people with different gifts, doing different liturgical ministries for the good of the whole body. Engaged participation is the action of the whole assembly in the liturgical event in such a way that each person is involved in the action according to his or her specific role in it. Throughout, it is helpful to safeguard the building's role in inviting persons to move and interact with each other. When the whole room is rigid and does not allow for movement, it sends the felt message that freedom and movement are not good.

  For example, after renewing the baptismal covenant, the assembly might approach the font, the people marking each other with the sign of the cross in water; or the scriptures might be passed among the people for veneration following the sermon (a practice of ancient synagogal origin); or the people might engage in a simple form of dance; or they may join the presider and other ministers during the eucharistic prayer, with arms open in the classic Christian position for prayer; or they may light each other's candles at the beginning of evening prayer and at the Easter Vigil.

- *Embodies a particular culture:* Since a good liturgical place has a flavor that says, "This is our place," it follows that every liturgical space will be somewhat different. The basic foci—assembly, ambo, font, and table—might be similar, but a Latino font will probably look different from a Scandinavian one. The worship place thus expresses the taste, ministry, culture, and interests of a particular congregation as something treasured and valued. The building says to the casual visitor, "We value who we are and what we do here."

- *Allows multiple uses:* The strict reservation of a space for one particular ritual function is neither necessary nor traditional. Our earliest gathering places were homes; later, medieval cathedrals served as market places in inclement weather. The same worship space might be used differently for different occasions, rendering a parish hall unnecessary, or freeing it for another purpose. Coffee hour, receptions, gatherings, banquets, and classes are highly appropriate in the worship space. This is an ancient custom going back to the many uses found in most synagogues, as well as the Christian tradition of not repeating the pagan distinction between sacred and profane, but disclosing in worship the sacredness of everything we thought profane. By the same token, a good worship space also encourages the congregation in its ministry to the surrounding world by facilitating the distribution of food and resources to the poor, the education of the ignorant, clothing the naked, etc., thus recovering the early Christian sense of liturgy as public service.
- *Supports the last, first:* A good worship space welcomes the participation of all: affirming the liturgical role of children, of other-abled persons, of the poor, the sick, the outcast and scapegoat; for, in their inclusion as vital elements, the Christian assembly is revealed as first fruits of the reign of God.

Becoming aware of the non-verbal, gut-level ways in which our gathering place communicates and forms us will assist us to address consciously the ways in which our gathering place expresses and gives rise to our feelings and attitudes about God, the world, ourselves, and what we envision God's reign of justice and peace to be. If we ignore the role of our gathering place in the formation of our attitudes, we will risk saying and understanding one thing while experiencing another. Until there is a congruence between what the liturgy claims to mean and what it embodies in the felt experience of the participants, our worship will not be an experience felt and done but rather something only understood abstractly.

Changing the Worship Space

Ritual is by nature conservative. We all have a need for a certain amount of predictability and sameness in liturgy. For this reason, changes in the worship space should take place over time, with plenty of discussion, and as a process of choosing among alternatives rather than accepting an enforced pattern. Even at its best, liturgical change is fraught with anxiety.

There is no change without anxiety. Given the lack of change in our liturgical places over the last hundred years, a move towards a better worship space is bound to create anxiety. The pastoral leadership of the parish must decide whether to protect the parishioners from change only to pass on the need for change till later, when the need—and also the anxiety—will be even greater, or to employ their pastoral skills to reassure and build up the congregation through the process.

The process of helping a congregation to reflect upon and design a new or remodeled worship space can be a thrilling and formative experience for all involved. The Church Building Fund (815 Second Avenue, New York, NY, 10017, PH: 800-334-7626) can provide expert assistance. Call to request their publications, including a process workbook and video program.

How to Tell a "Good News" Place

- You are not just welcomed; you are invited in.
- You are expected.
- Your thoughts and modes of expression are valued.
- You can see and hear everything that is happening.
- You can move around to greet, talk with others.
- The distinctions in liturgical roles are articulated without the implication that some are more worthy than others.
- The space is sturdy; it can handle being used by people.
- Architecturally it is crafted with care and professional artistry.
- It looks best when full and being used.

Creating Art for Worship

by Ralph Carskadden

In former times it was said that "the iconography of Anglicanism is verbal." As Anglicans, we used to define ourselves by words and texts used in our corporate worship. But we now live in what may be called a "post-Guttenberg" age, a time when words have lost much of their power to define and communicate. And, if words have lost some of their power, signs, symbols, and actions have not. Indeed, as we know, our actions speak louder than our words. And so, the current Book of Common Prayer provides more rubrical directions for actions than any previous book, and contains a long list of material things which are either *required* for worship (water, wine, bread, fair linens) or *may* be used in worship (incense, candles, vesture, oil, etc.).

The place of symbols, signs, and actions in liturgical worship is central to our understanding and celebration of the sacramental nature of the Christian faith because the "outward and visible" is capable of conveying "inward and spiritual grace." In our time, we are again coming to understand that the fuller the sacramental sign and action, the more fully our perception and understanding of the grace can be (not that the grace itself is greater, of course!).

As we consider the important role the non-musical arts play in our worship, it is good to remember that the liturgy itself—the actions, words, and gestures of the people of God in worship—is the primary art form. For this action by the gathered people, the architects provide a physical space, metalworkers and glassblowers and potters provide vessels, carpenters and woodworkers craft furniture, weavers and needleworkers provide clothing for the altar, banners for processions, and garments for various ministers. Glassworkers can bring their skills with windows, capturing natural light and releasing it to beautify, teach, and edify. Sculptors and painters can enhance the worship environment with statues and icons. And to this list could be added the art of the dance.

Reflection on a few of these art forms can encourage our exploration of others and help us understand the vital role the arts potentially play in communicating and celebrating faith.

Dance

We begin by keeping in mind the movements suggested by the Prayer Book—the entrance of people and ministers, movement of readers to and from the "word place," the procession of the gifts during the offertory, and the procession to and from the place of communion by the assembly. On special days such as the Sunday of the Passion, there is the movement of the whole people from a place of gathering where the palm liturgy takes place to the church. At baptisms there is a procession to the "water place." Also, during the liturgy the community uses posture to communicate the nature of what is taking place and the role of the assembly in the action. Our current Prayer Book restores standing as an ancient posture of corporate prayer and praise. The community usually sits to listen to lessons and sermons, and may kneel, especially for prayers of confession and penitence. These movements and their accompanying gestures are an art form, the community of faith a kind of *corps de ballet.* To the movement of the whole assembly would be added the movement of particular ministers, as individuals and as teams in the liturgy: acolytes, deacons and presiders, lay eucharistic ministers, and musicians. Finally, in addition to these considerations there could be movement by a few specially trained people who have come to be known as "liturgical dancers." [Ed. note: see "Jesus Wants to Dance!—in Church—with US!!!," by Richard Fabian, on page 71].

Vessels

Influenced by the liturgical movement of the last thirty years, many congregations are returning to the primitive practice of immersion for baptism, leavened bread for the eucharist and fuller use of oil for chrismation and anointing the sick. If we are going to use enough water to immerse a candidate (always the first option in every Book of Common Prayer since 1549) then what form will be the vessel that contains the water? What size will it need to be? How will it be filled? And how will it be emptied? If bread is really going to be broken, then what form will the bread take? Remember the culinary arts. Are there ethnic or regional bread-baking traditions that could be considered? What form will the vessel take that holds real bread? What about oil for chrism or oil for anointing? At baptism a little dab won't do for the anointing of new royal, holy, priestly, servant people! The psalmist suggests that such anointings are marked by an abundance of fragrant oil. What vessel and what gestures can inform our decisions? The old architectural slogan "form follows function" can help us discern these things. Clarify your needs, then look in unexpected places like kitchen shops, import stores, and crafts fairs. If you don't find what you need, check the local colleges and universities for an artist who could be commissioned to make the objects and vessels you need. Support and encourage local talent wherever possible. Affirm your region and the crafts traditions of your area. We don't live in England anymore.

Textiles

We have gone through three decades of banner-making in the church. Much of what was made reflected group process and enthusiasm, and the products of these efforts served well for a time or occasion. But too often those temporary creations were treated as permanent art, which they were not. At a time when many congregations noticed that their worship environment was drab or dull, the banner explosion *did* add a note of color. But frequently those efforts were left on display all year and they became part of visual clutter and created a pastoral problem of what to do with things that were unable to survive long-term use and scrutiny.

Before crafts people begin to work, it is important to set some priorities and standards. First of all, apply their efforts to the main focal points of our worship. Make full coverings for the holy table or altar which vest the Lord's table with dignity and beauty and provide for change of color from season to season, giving strong, clear evidence of the unfolding drama of redemption through the liturgical year. After the altar is vested with a frontal and full fair linen (this is a banquet table), then consider a hanging for the "word place," be it a lectern or pulpit. Provide more than the "traditional" postage stamp or a change in the "color of suspenders on the eagle," as Dr. Boone Porter quipped, referring to the usual Bible markers.

Second, distinguish between temporary and lasting furnishings. For single occasions, a felt-and-glue banner might work well. For longer use, permanent techniques need to be employed. Use the best workmanship for things which are meant to last. This is work for the house of God!

Third, explore the wide range of colors which have been or could be used. Don't limit yourself to just the late Roman sequence of white, red, green, and purple. Advent has a fine tradition of blue as well as purple—perhaps use both. Festal might be white but the right yellow or mixture of colors might be more appropriate in your space. (In Japan white is a color for mourning.)

Are there ethnic or regional considerations for color or weave, texture or pattern which might be helpful in your congregation. (St. Margaret's, Bellevue, Washington, has a great tartan frontal!) In England, Lent was marked by the use of unbleached linen ornamented with blood- red and black. It seems a much more appropriate option than purple or violet which are often the most visually impressive colors you can use. Holy Week of course is now a blood-red or deep-red color suggestive of Jesus as the king of martyrs. For the feast of Pentecost, you can continue the Easter colors or explode in fire with reds, oranges, and yellows.

Fourth, it is important to realize that we don't need slogans or texts on our work. The materials we use should themselves have "presence." They should speak clearly about what they are. Texture and color and form and shape communicate to us. Large, ample, colorful garments can signify an order of ministry, a season in the year of grace, and the region or peoples who are gathered to celebrate. The garments themselves, if well made of good materials, are symbolic. They do not need ecclesiastical signs or symbols tacked on in order to be used in the liturgy.

Fifth, explore the best skills at hand. Glorious quilts are being made everywhere. (One of the most stunning frontals I made was a patchwork of Thai silks in blues and greens.) Fine old stitches are being rediscovered, and, with the newer machines, many members—male and female—can do appliqué and construction of vesture. Weavers of great skill can be found around the country. Many colleges and universities are training students to screen and print on fabric. With the number of talented and well-trained craftspeople available, handsome altar coverings, paraments, and vestments can be made locally.

Sixth, consider what might be especially appropriate for your region or the peoples who make up your faith community. A business partner and I operated an ecclesiastical textile studio for twenty years providing vesture, frontals, and banners. Some of our most exciting work was in response to the needs of congregations wanting to signify in some way their ethnic or cultural heritage. At the Church of the Intercession in New York City, we did a set of West African-inspired festal vestments using Kente cloth patterns which were batiked onto silk and ornamented with gold kid leather designs based on Adinkira designs. For St. Clement's, Seattle, a racially-mixed parish where I now serve as rector, the altar frontals are of rich Thai silk ornamented with vivid bands of Kente cloth. When Vincent Warner became Bishop of Olympia here in the Northwest, we commissioned a local artist who works in North Coast Native-American style to create a descending dove in an equal-armed cross for the ordination ceremony. The design was worked in red, white, blue, and green with pearl buttons for an altar frontal. The same design was worked in silver and enamel for Bishop Warner's cross, and, in the years since, it has been screened on T-shirts and forms the logo for the diocesan newspaper. It fits the area, and people are clear that it somehow signifies the church in this region.

Imaging Faith

A word about images. I have served as a consultant to many churches across the country. Recently I visited a very large parish in the South where I met with the altar guild which had just finished a very ambitious needlework project for a children's chapel. It was a needlepoint tapestry of Jesus and the children. With great pride, they took me to the chapel to see the fruits of their labor. The stitches were impeccable. The scale of the design was good. But there was Jesus, as big as life, surrounded by all white children. In their enthusiasm for their project, no one had thought about what the tapestry would communicate about Jesus. He was clearly Anglo-Saxon as were all the children. This in a city renowned for Dr. Martin Luther King's best efforts. We must let the images of humans in our windows, icons, and statues reflect the full spectrum of the communion of saints. It is imperative that we use the arts to communicate on every level the breadth of God's inclusive grace and love. The cloth and designs we use, the patterns and colors and forms need to reflect the worldwide Communion of which we are part.

With these things in mind, perhaps we can better appreciate the role of the arts in worship. They give us alternate languages to speak of realities seen as well as realities unseen. In the diverse tongues of dance and poetry, music and painting, woven cloth and beaten metal, carved wood and shaped clay, we can respond to our experience of God and give voice and vision to life in the kingdom. And because these alternate—and often ancient—languages are so important, let us be bold in our use of them. The Prayer Book suggests that it is desirable to use "books of appropriate size and dignity" (a reasonable suggestion from a church whose iconography has been verbal!) and so it follows that all of our vessels, signs, symbols, gestures, vesture, and liturgical buildings need also to be of suitable size and dignity!

The Role of the Arts in the Liturgical Assembly

by Marilyn L. Haskel

> ... music in Christian worship is an embodied form of praying. Liturgy is inherently musical. That is, it involves speaking, listening, movement, and rest—all of which [are] rhythmic and [have] pitch, intensity, and tonal register. Attunement to the pace, rhyme and tacit "music" of heightened speech in prayer and proclamation is crucial to participation in the ritual dimensions of the liturgy.[18]

To speak of the *role* of music, drama, dance, and art in the liturgical assembly can be misleading. To speak in this way about the arts in liturgy is to assign a character to them much as a person becomes a character in a play. A character's job (role) may be to advance the action, to contribute information to the story line, to add humor or pathos to the plot, or to round out the balance of the universal appeal of the cast. Misunderstanding occurs when it is assumed that "liturgy" or a liturgical form is an order of words in which symbolic sound, movement, action, or visual representation is cast in the role of enhancing or decorating this order of words. This assumption separates the inherent nature of liturgy into false components that could be selectively pruned in the interest of time constraints or theological discourse.

One doesn't have to belabor Don Saliers's characterization of liturgy as "inherently musical" to draw parallels to drama, dance, and the visual arts. Liturgy is also inherently dramatic; it dances; and it is visually artistic.

During this time of liturgical reform, it is easy to believe that what we are called to do as artists is to add contemporary versions of our respective arts to the new prayer forms, thereby creating a contemporary liturgical "experience." We may be seduced into thinking that our liturgies must look, feel, and sound exclusively like our everyday world if they are to attract the unchurched or have any meaning for young, fast-track adults, not to mention children and youth. This interest in the purely contemporary has rendered the word "traditional" a derogatory label for anything created prior to the 1960s or associated with a conservative segment of the population. What we lose—if we

[18]Saliers, Don E., "The Integrity of Sung Prayer," Worship, July 1981, p. 292

subscribe to this traditional/contemporary dichotomy—are the global possibilities of embracing both heritage *and* vision.

We may be tempted to believe that, if a pseudo-artistic gloss on our liturgies doesn't elicit an emotional response, then, spiritually, the liturgy isn't working. Conversely, it is curious that the value our society places on illusory and shallow emotional responses to the full spectrum of life's drama lures us into avoiding the poignant honesty of evoking the extremes of either agony or ecstasy in our worship. Our range of emotional response becomes limited to feeling "sad," "depressed," "happy," "comfortable," or "uplifted" when we gather for worship.

The arts *can* be manipulative and intrusive by giving worship a "day-glo" sheen which is merely entertaining or titillating. This can "get them in the door" for a time, but ultimately it will not support a spiritual way of living. Inherently artistic liturgy, on the other hand, is authentic and vital prayer. It is this tension between what the arts *can* do *to* liturgy and what they *must* do *within* liturgy that makes some of the clergy and laity ambivalent toward the artist's contribution. This ambivalence stems from a concern about what motivates us artists to do what we do. Because our motives probably *aren't* the usual ones—e.g., financial gain or job security—some people fear that our motivation may be a far more dangerous "vice": *power* that is fed by the worship of art alone. As artists, we are conversant with a powerful medium, the intricacies of which are minimally understood by some; therefore, it is important that our skills be refined not only by the disciplines of our craft, but also by the disciplines of the gospel. This dual discipline must be readily observable by all. As Christians it is our witness. Don Saliers is again helpful:

> If we settle for the pompous, the grandiose, or romantically self-assertive, how heavy and pompous will be our experience of corporate prayer. Our precocious complexity can often make our faith experience in liturgy difficult and cluttered. This is why the search for adequate musical forms is problematic: precisely because it is so easy to confuse depth of emotion with intensity of immediate feeling. Music has the capacity to express the morphology of our "felt experience" of the world, as Suzanne Langer and others have pointed out. . . . Do we settle for the conventional or the comfortable, conforming to the 'musical tastes' of the people? *Or*, do we enter into those praisings, repentings, hopings; those longings, rejoicings and thankings which are peculiar to the heart of the Christian Gospel?[19]

If music, as well as the other arts, has the capacity to express the form or structure of our felt experience of the world, clergy and laity want to be assured that artists working in the church understand and acknowledge that their art is not the supreme message, but rather a *bearer* of the supreme message.

A textbook definition of liturgy might say that we gather to glorify God, to hear and proclaim the good news, to profess belief, to pray, to recall and celebrate the death and

[19]Ibid. p. 293

resurrection of Jesus, and, being strengthened and renewed, to go forth into the world to witness all that we know and believe about our lives in Christ, calling others to do the same. And this definition is right. This *is* what we *do*. But what we want to ***happen*** in liturgy is that we learn who we are as the body of Christ. We are to become radically committed to Christ, and thus, to each other in the world. We are to encounter the face of the world in the face of God, become transformed and transforming, entering the critical dialogue of word and sacrament; and in so doing, we lust after the time when the *dis-ease* of the world is so abhorrent to us that we must love it unto death.

This can't be accomplished by cute or pedestrian means. The gospel is frightening and freeing in its radical insistence on commitment. There isn't a lite or decaffeinated version. The gospel requires full-bodied, cross-your-heart, holistically-demanding commitment. Anemic rituals and clever rhymes won't bear the weight of it. Only liturgy that grabs our hearts with both hands and wrings complacency from our bones will gird us throughout life-journeys with the ever-increasing surety of our membership in the body of Christ.

Becoming the body isn't a matter of "filling up on fervor" or escaping the world into the pseudo-mystical. Quite simply, it is the dance of "being ourselves, telling the truth and stepping out."[20] In liturgy we hear the story, claim our own, name the sin, offer and accept forgiveness, thank God, and grasp the outstretched hand of need in each other by offering ourselves to the world.

In the exercise of rites and rituals, we seek not only to renew our commitment to ministry, but also to enter more deeply into our relationship to God. We are dependent on the liturgy to help us make the connections between our lives in this world and the gospel's requirement of us. We are dependent on the liturgy and its environment to help us fulfill our need for transcendence and beauty. And finally, we are dependent on the liturgy to affirm us in our journey.

There is a television station that has an ad campaign which claims, "You have questions; Five has answers." In a time when the computer that helped put us on the moon has one-tenth of the capacity of the average home computer today, people have come to demand such quickly stated solutions. "Life is short (fast ?); just tell us what to do."

Seeking Christian answers to the questions of life is a highly motivating force in bringing people to church. As the body of Christ, we proclaim that we "have answers." Clergy are expected to communicate answers by preaching well. Some people want sermons that answer questions about the historical facts of scripture read that day; others want the priest to clearly outline "Lifestyles of the Spiritually Rich and Famous" (including the priest's!); still others want a good story with a meaningful message.

---

[20]A quote from the Rev. Dr. Minka Sprague's concluding address to the Association of Diocesan Liturgy and Music Commissions, 1993.

Do we expect the service of the word—the scripture readings and the sermon—to be the sole medium for communicating the "answers"? Is it realistic to expect that direct communication to the person in the pew—just "telling them what to do"—will form people adequately and passionately for the work of the gospel?

A symbol is that which points to a truth beyond itself or which represents something greater than its own immediate meaning. The cross is a symbol for Christians because, beyond its physical appearance and its use for criminal punishment, it represents the entire drama of Jesus' death and subsequent resurrection. It communicates a truth of great magnitude in its simplicity.

The arts: music, drama, dance, painting, architecture, and sculpture are forms of communication that are highly symbolic. The arts point to a truth which lies beyond themselves.

Language is also a symbolic communication in that it is a configuration of letters that construct words which, when combined, are capable of the transfer of information. Letters and words stand for something else. Language can be more than a vehicle of direct communication. The combination of words and phrases can be so constructed as to be art. Poetry is such art. The language of the 1928 Book of Common Prayer is high prose, another such art. The text in "Cranmer English" communicated far more than the content of the words. For many people these sounds, the ideas verbalized as well as the physical sensation of saying them, profoundly embodied what they believed not only theologically but ideologically.

Similarly, the architectural design of a church building may communicate that it is a church. Seeing it in its physical setting may evoke a sense of invitation, warmth, and openness. A good design, however, will go even further by inviting one into a continuing experience of perception and discernment as one's relationship continues with the building.

It is this ability of the arts to escape the realm of "direct idea" communication that enables us to do the spiritual, transforming work of discerning the gospel. Art seeks not to be a communicator of cheap emotion and easy interpretation, but rather to engage each of us in our own language of knowing and to enable us to continue searching for that deeper well of life-giving water. Art is a vehicle which helps us make the discovery that Christ is here and now and encourages us to tell others.

Preaching and Praying the Lectionary:
Letting the Lectionary Set the Agenda for the Congregation in Planning and Celebrating the Eucharist

by Joseph P. Russell

"As we seek to understand and interpret scripture, we need the perspective of others in the group, the wisdom acquired over the centuries, the knowledge of biblical scholarship and the influence of the rhythm of corporate worship," writes Linda Grenz in the Episcopal Church Center publication *In Dialogue with Scripture: An Episcopal Guide to Studying the Bible.*[21] "An important principle of bible study is this: Two people in Dialogue over the text bring twice the potential for discovery that the single person working alone does. Group study can enhance the discovery process as members of the group share insights and questions."[22]

Too often the worship for the congregation is planned by the priest alone, or at best by the priest meeting briefly with the musician. The celebrant opens Bible, commentary, and a lectionary preparation resource and plans the Sunday liturgy in the privacy of the office. Sometimes the bulletins and sermon from three years ago form the basis for much of the present year's planning. The storage and retrieval features of personal computers have tempted many of us to use cut-and-paste methods and save the time of planning from scratch. But if liturgy is truly to be "the work of the people," and if liturgy is to express the prayer and praise of the congregation at a particular moment in time, then the people who worship will ideally be involved in the hard work of designing and preparing the liturgy as well as participating in the end product of the preparation!

The process starts with the lectionary texts and a group of worshipers who come together for study and dialogue around those texts. In a small congregation, the group can be three or four people who form a midweek Bible study and prayer group. Planning the worship may give the group a whole new lease on life. Where several small congrega-

---

[21] *In Dialogue With Scripture: An Episcopal Guide to Studying the Bible*, Linda Grenz, ed., is published by the Episcopal Church Center to encourage effective Bible study and dialogue.

[22]Ibid., p. 6.

tions have joined together in a cluster for worship and ministry, the planning team can involve one or two people from each congregation. Catechumens and reaffirmers participating in the congregation's catechumenal process could plan the Sunday worship occasionally.

The key leaders of the liturgy will be involved, of course, but their participation in the group planning will be to listen as much as to direct. Ideally, those who plan the liturgy will also share in the leadership of the worship as well. Out of the planning group come the intercessor, lectors, catechists, choir members, and others. The membership of the planning group needs to shift from time to time. Again, the goal is to make liturgical planning "the work of the people." If that is to work, then as many of the people of the congregation as possible need to be part of the process. One way of assuring a change of membership would be to form the groups around planning for a specific season. For example, as the liturgical year winds down, a new planning group is formed to shape the worship for Advent through the First Sunday after the Epiphany. The members are given a crash course in liturgical planning that includes the traditions and theological themes associated with their given season. From that beginning, they move to the week-by-week planning process.

The convener of the group needs to describe the context of the scripture readings so that participants can see the relationship between the readings and the psalm, and understand the tradition that lies behind text and placement in the lectionary. Because three texts are probably going to be more than the group will be able to handle creatively, the focus of dialogue will often be narrowed to one of the texts, usually the gospel.

The following adaptation of one of the Bible study methods found in the resource *In Dialogue* is an example of a process that may help the group move from text, to life and ministry, to liturgy design.

Questions for Dialogue

What did you hear?

- Write three thoughts, ideas, phrases, images that struck you in these readings.

What did it mean?

- Why do you think these words/phrases struck you today? What do they mean for your life and for the witness of this congregation to the world?
- Can you recall a time in your life (past or present) when you experienced something similar to the event expressed in these readings? How do these readings enlighten or challenge that experience?

- How does this text (these texts) confront or affirm the witness we are making as the church in light of the baptismal covenant.
    - Will you continue in the apostles' teaching and fellowship, in the breaking of the bread, and in the prayers?
    - Will you persevere in resisting evil, and, whenever you fall into sin, repent and return to the Lord?
    - Will you proclaim by word and example the good news of God in Christ?
    - Will you seek and serve Christ in all persons, loving your neighbor as yourself?
    - Will you strive for justice and peace among all people, and respect the dignity of every human being?
- Write three issues that these readings raise for you as you think about the planning of the worship.

Given our dialogue, how shall we celebrate the eucharist together?

- How shall we gather? (entrance rite)
- How shall we proclaim the word? (reading, preaching, singing, dancing the texts)
- How shall we pray? (prayers of the people)
- How shall we offer the eucharistic prayer? (choices of one of the eucharistic prayers at the principal Sunday or weekly celebration of the eucharist or the writing of the eucharistic prayer at other times)
- How shall we sing our praise? (choice of hymns and canticles)
- How shall we go forth into the world? (the dismissal)

As the group reflect on their experience with the lectionary texts, the planning task becomes clearer. Scripture dialogue leads to the choice of eucharistic prayer as well as to the choice of hymns; to the writing or adapting of the prayers of the people as well as to the bulletin cover. [23]

We may not be able to do this kind of planning every time we worship, but the experience of planning together will influence the way the congregation celebrates the liturgy in subtle ways. The solo planner becomes more sensitive to how others may read the texts from the experience of hearing the ideas and concerns when the group planning was done. If the process seems time consuming, remember that the group planning can

[23] An excellent resource to assist in the writing of prayers of the people is *Intercessions for The Christian People*, Gail Ramshaw, ed., Liturgical Press, 1988. We are not limited to the six forms of the prayers of the people found on pages 383–393 of the Prayer Book. The rubric is deliberately permissive in regard to the forms of intercession. "Any of the forms which follow may be used. . . . Adaptations or insertions suitable to the occasion may be made."

expedite sermon preparing, hymn selections and enhance the ministry of lector, intercessor, and other liturgical leaders. The time and energy spent with a group may expedite the rest of the necessary planning steps. The preacher leaves with some hymn or anthem choices already made. The lector feels familiar enough with the texts to offer them with conviction.

The catechumenal process is having a remarkable effect on congregational life and worship. Historically, the lectionary was developed out of the need to evangelize, catechize, convert, and equip the people who were coming into the church. The assigned texts for Lent in Years A and B are a short course in the meaning of our baptism. Each week of Lent touches on another aspect of the baptismal rite. The lections for the Great Fifty Days of Easter lead the congregation into a reflection on how they will know the risen Christ in their lives, and how they will make Christ known in the world around them. The lections for the Sundays after the Feast of the Epiphany focus on the calling and formation of Jesus' disciples. How appropriate those texts are for us as we work with catechumens, reaffirmers, and, indeed, the whole congregation today!

If we keep the catechumenal process in mind as we think about the planning of the liturgy week by week, we find our preaching and design preparation flowing far more smoothly. To focus the five weeks of Lent on the sacrament of baptism gives us a direction of preaching, added insights for those involved in the catechumenal process, and an involvement of the whole congregation in the deepening of faith and commitment that comes out of process. As mentioned above, it may be the catechumens and reaffirmers who will help to give shape to the congregation's liturgy. Their own spiritual pilgrimage, their own deepening commitment to their baptismal vows, may find expression in the prayers and praises of the whole congregation.

Ideally, the congregation's worship reflects the lections appointed for the occasion from entrance rite to words of dismissal. For example, the way the entrance rite is carried out can vary depending on the sense and feeling of the lessons. A triumphant note of joy expressed in the gospel text may lead to a full procession with entrance hymn on one Sunday, while a gospel reading reflecting the call to share in the cross may lead to a silent entrance of liturgical leaders followed by the greeting between celebrant and people and an intoned "Lord have mercy."

Contrast this kind of flexible planning with the practice of picking a eucharistic prayer or form of the prayers of the people and using that form over a long period of time. The Prayer Book offers options so that each experience of worship can more adequately express the biblical texts as well as the life of the congregation. One of the reasons we sometimes hesitate to use the fullness of the Prayer Book is our concern about confusing the worshipers who have enough trouble as it is finding their way around the Prayer Book. Printing the necessary congregational responses in the bulletin, however, can eliminate the need for people to be always on the "right page" of the Prayer Book.

Simply print the cue sentence from the Prayer Book along with the appropriate response. A worship leader can help to lead the congregation in their responses, making it easier for them to participate.

As the calendar leads us beyond the Day of Pentecost (or "ordinary time" as the Roman Catholics call the counted weeks), one may find that this is a time when preachers can become dry and planning groups can run out of steam as the relaxed sense of summer meets a lectionary without major landmarks and celebrations.

If we see the counted Sundays after Pentecost as one long, serialized reading from the gospel of the year, however, the "long green season," as it is sometimes called, may take on a new life. During the summer in Year A, we hear two discourses of Jesus dealing with discipleship and a series of parables shedding light on the kingdom of heaven. Two narrative sections are also heard in which there is growing rejection of Jesus as he begins to reveal his messiahship and the nature of the church. In Year B, our summer is highlighted with Mark's account of Jesus' travels in Galilee and, then, his visits to Nazareth, the Sea of Galilee, Bethsaida, Tyre, Sidon, and so forth. The preacher can use the journeys to build momentum and continuity for summer preaching and liturgical planning. Luke leads us on a solemn journey to Jerusalem in Year C, beginning with Proper 8, the Sunday closest to June 29th. We walk with Jesus on that foreboding journey right through to the first week of November. Here we begin to see the shadow of the Cross fall ever more ominously across the path that Jesus and his followers are walking. The lectionary texts preached in the context of that journey take on a new urgency.

The epistles are also read sequentially during the season after Pentecost, so here again we have the opportunity to move in serialized fashion through the great writings of the New Testament. One week builds on the week before. It is like watching a mini-series on television. There can always be a "to be continued" sense to preaching and to the shaping of the liturgy. Of course this semi-continuity of epistles and gospel will be lost to the occasional worshiper, but that need not deter liturgical planners and leaders from immersing themselves in the unfolding story over the course of the weeks of "ordinary time." The sense of movement and journey could be heightened for the congregation with bulletin boards and marked out maps of the journey. As the lectionary leads into the opening chapters of an epistle, locate Philippi or Corinth with a map on the bulletin cover or a sign by the door of the nave that says, "Welcome to Corinth. Join St. Paul for six weeks as we read his First Letter to the Corinthians." A poster could list well known quotations from First Corinthians with a headline saying, "Listen for these familiar sayings and see how they fit then and now."

If there are Bible study groups meeting in the congregation, the obvious focus will be the lections for the coming week, the appointed gospel for the year, or the epistle that will be heard in serialized readings in the coming weeks. A seminar on the Gospel

According to Mark in the weeks leading up to Advent in Year B, for example, is a way to engage a group in the gospel they will be hearing for the next year.

As we concentrate on preaching and praying the lectionary as it is published in the Book of Common Prayer, it is important to keep in mind developments taking place in the larger church. *The Revised Common Lectionary*, produced by the Consultation on Common Texts and published in this country by Abingdon Press, is an effort to unify lectionaries used by a growing number of denominations in this country, including the Disciples of Christ, Christian Reformed Church in North America, the Episcopal Church, the Evangelical Lutheran Church in America, the Roman Catholic Church, the Lutheran Church - Missouri Synod, the Polish National Catholic Church, the Presbyterian Church (U.S.A.), the Reformed Church in America, Unitarian Universalist Christian Fellowship, the United Church of Christ, and the United Methodist Church. Though the lectionary is optional in most of those denominations, the growing interest and use of a lectionary offers unparalleled opportunities for everything from ecumenical Bible studies to shared education and preaching resources. For example, the United Church of Christ recently has completed work on a major new curriculum based on *The Revised Common Lectionary*.[24]

The lectionary follows the familiar three-year pattern of appointed readings in which the Old Testament lection and psalm are in thematic harmony with the gospel. An option is offered during the Sundays after Pentecost, however. Liturgists may choose to follow a series of sequential readings from the Old Testament so that the congregation hears the unfolding story of the Old Testament in context. Old Testament lections in thematic harmony with the gospel are also offered as an alternative. Texts that highlight the role of women in the Bible that are not included in the present Prayer Book lectionary are heard with *The Revised Common Lectionary*. Additional lections from the Wisdom literature offer the opportunity to hear an attribute of God referred to as feminine: "Does not Wisdom call, and does not understanding raise her voice? On the heights, beside the way, at the crossroads she takes her stand; beside the gates in front of the town, at the entrance of the portals she cries out ... " (Proverbs 8:1–3, Trinity Sunday, Year C, *The Revised Common Lectionary*).

Liturgy: the work of the people. May our liturgy truly reflect the struggle, the vision, and the hopes of the people as their experience with text and life is reflected in how the worship is offered each time the congregation gathers to hear God's word and to respond in prayer, in praise, and in sacrament.

[24]*The Inviting Word*, United Church Press. Complete curriculum, including three volumes of lection-based commentaries and age-level leader and learner guides.

Jesus Wants to Dance!—In Church!!—With Us!!!

by Richard Fabian

Dance and worship have been long married. Once constant company, they appear together rarely now, and keep different sets of friends. At the rare church feasts when all gather, their friends nod or smile, but barely mix; the worshipers watch the dancers awhile; then the dancers step aside and the worshipers resume feasting in their accustomed way. Such estrangement wants explaining. Outside church, these same worshipers dance readily enough; and inside church, everyone talks of celebration today. Why then is Christian worship still so far from the talk of Jesus, whose Aramaic tongue said "rejoice" by using the verb "to dance?"

Longtime puritan anxiety is one cause. As a young warrior, King David joined up with roving prophet bands, who harped and psalmed and danced naked on stony Judean hillsides. He shocked aristocrats when he brought his prophetic bodily style into royal worship (2 Samuel 6); but only a little better clothed, music and dance flowered at court and temple for centuries thereafter. By contrast, Christians emerging from the persecutions into Roman civic eminence adopted wholesale the Roman educated classes' disgust at popular revelry. J. G. Davies describes preachers' campaigns from the fourth century onward to purge dancing from Christian life (see "For Further Reading," page 153ff.). Like pagan Hellenistic thinkers, these crusaders saw our human bodies as our chief human problem, and feared dance and song alike as alarmingly sensuous. Fourth- and fifth-century sermons show ambivalence, at best, toward music and dance, sometimes extolling them—but rarely inside the liturgy. Bishops like Augustine introduced congregational singing only as a last resort, to keep unruly crowds from talking during services. Dance in church found even fewer pulpit or conciliar champions. In a backhand way, the many centuries of church canons against Christian dancing prove its hardy popularity despite these crusades. But for most of eastern Christendom, dance became lay people's stuff, celebrated in home courtyards or village squares *outside* the church. That is how Greek and Arab Christians dance today; and Moslems across Asia and Africa have followed suit.

Dance and worship held hands together longer elsewhere. To this day, Ethiopians —the largest eastern church—enjoy clergy dancing after Sunday services, and congregational dancing on festivals; and Russian clergy still dance at Easter mattins. Throughout the medieval west, as well, church dances by clergy and layfolk sprang up both inside and outside the liturgy, and endured hardily. Indeed, western church dance bloomed for so long that modern scholars are often surprised to learn how recently it withered. For example, literary commentators on Dante's *Paradiso* wonder silently now when Dante spies a circle of humming lights and straightway meets Thomas Aquinas. Dante expected his readers to recognize the celebrated spectacle of theologians dancing in circles, in his day their most public activity, and a university custom still seen in eighteenth-century Cambridge, where aging Doctors of Divinity gathered each spring in bright red robes to dance around the new doctoral candidates. Indeed, though the reformation launched fresh waves of puritan opprobrium, driving dance from western cathedrals and parish churches, yet on the margins of that same reformation, Calvinist revivalists and Shakers completed their worship with dancing and marching well into the nineteenth century.

After so long a history, worship leaders might expect to recover congregational dancing easily, just as ballroom couples today are rediscovering the Latin American rhythms popular a few decades ago, before rock-and-roll drove them from the dance floor. But few Christians have done so—and here is the second cause for the remarkable estrangement in our churches—because we have lost our long-loved models for congregational dance, and must make them anew.

Writing dances down is a modern idea, much younger than musical notation; so we have been losing dances for ages. Hebrew temple music and dance became secret arts, soon forgotten after Roman armies wrecked Herod's temple and paved it over to wipe out all memory. In the fourth century, Gregory Nazianzus applauded congregations dancing at Easter, trampling death underfoot: a gesture cited in the Easter refrain *(troparion)* still popularly sung at Eastern Orthodox Eastertide services, and now gracing page 500 of the Episcopal Prayer Book. But only a few secular mosaics survive to suggest what steps patristic Christians actually danced. Their music has vanished, and, with it, the rhythm, tempo, gestures, and feel.

Medieval western Christians caroled enthusiastically at festivals—and the French word "carol," like the Greek "chorus," meant dancing first of all. Moreover, Renaissance hymns based on popular ditties almost beg to be danced again today. But these popular steps, too, are largely lost, despite the work of renaissance dance masters who were our earliest dance chroniclers, noting down their courtly variations. Gymnastic and fashionably complex, these variations defy congregational use today. They evolved into baroque court and theater dance and, then, into classical ballet; concurrently, the popular, social dancing steps evolved into cotillions and reels. Soon layfolk and clergy alike danced only in ballrooms and mostly in couples, until dancing served romance and courtship, but no longer prayer or community rejoicing. At the same time, Shaker dances, though they kept their communal religious character, were purposely made hard to do. Shakers wanted to experience the body's limitations before fleeing them, ultimately, in death; so they designed awkward movements, impractical for popular use. For so many reasons, European tradition provides scant resource for reviving congregational dance now.

Our own century has seen the "modern dance" revolution pioneered by Isadora Duncan, Martha Graham, Ruth St. Denis, Ted Shawn, and others. Here natural body movements made steps easier to imitate and new dances easier to design. Some creative churches and synagogues have introduced modern dance into their worship, training soloists and dance choirs to perform much as organists and singing choirs perform; meanwhile, the people watch and participate inwardly, or may be taught simple accompanying gestures. Modern dance can certainly enrich parish liturgy, by allowing volunteers a chance to develop their talents for dancing and share these with their fellow Christians on the sidelines. But the need for choreography, training, and rehearsal makes modern dance essentially performance dance, and—despite its popularity on stage—congregations have taken slowly to it. Though the movements may be natural, few watchers join in, even when a simple congregational part is offered them.

Such reluctant participation from people who dance readily enough outside church frustrates worship leaders' best intentions. Perhaps it results from overturning the normal relation between soloists and the crowd, when choreographers teach congregations simple movements to accompany the performers. Normally, solo dance develops as a specialization of popular dance and builds on known popular forms. (Rock-and-roll concerts show that relationship clearly: the audience take up familiar, unchoreographed movements, while the musicians on stage lead them with dramatic variations. Popular participation is never a problem here!) Moreover, most modern dance is interpretive; and interpretation can distract from liturgical action as much as illuminate it. For that very reason, "instructed eucharists" have lost currency, as churches found that the spoken interpretations interfered with people's participation in the liturgical actions themselves.

By contrast, recent videotapes by Thomas Kane show an exciting folk revival underway in African congregations, where the whole church joins in dancing during processions, canticles, and prayers. Here, instead of merely *interpreting* the entry processional texts, the dancing clergy and people *are* the entry procession, moving together in steps with rich traditional associations. African church dance engages the congregation by invoking folk dance movements known to everyone: something American modern dance cannot do—except in Latino or African-American parishes—because our European ethnic majority have lost touch with their communal dancing roots. To engage most parishioners in congregational dance today, we must supply a new folk-like vocabulary, quickly picked up, repetitive rather than interpretive, and flexible enough to serve many texts and tunes without elaborate memorization. Over the past quarter century, an ethnic folk dance movement has sprouted across North America, promising fresh resources for parish worship, and church dance leaders have begun to harvest these.

This author serves a San Francisco parish that is pioneering congregational dancing based on folk resources. Like our metropolitan ministry area, we combine contributions from different ethnic groups, welcoming what best fits our task. We are lucky to have thriving local dance companies to learn from, and an ethnic dance festival that grows bigger each year. Perhaps our work to date can serve other churches, too. St. Gregory Nyssen Church numbers a hundred worshipers on Sundays, and some three hundred at Easter. Building on the fondness Episcopalians already have for hymn-singing, we dance hymns to folk steps chosen because they exhibit the very qualities described above: quickly learned; repetitive; and fitting many texts and tunes. We dance these steps two or three times each Sunday, beginning and ending the eucharistic banquet. And on Easter, we dance them much more.

Our simplest steps come from opposite world hemispheres. *Tripudium* (three steps forward and one back; sometimes counted five steps forward and two back) was known in Europe from at least the eighth century, and survives today in annual processions at Echternach in Luxembourg. At the midpoint of every St. Gregory's service, our whole congregation dance *Tripudium,* processing to the altar and circling the table counter-clockwise until the hymn ends. The kiss of peace and Great Thanksgiving prayer follow at once, with all gathered round the table. From Africa comes *High Life,* an even simpler pattern (step sideways right, slide the left foot together, then step sideways left, and slide the right foot together). *High Life* is danced in place with a swing in the hips and knees, and sometimes a hand clap; American black gospel choirs dance it with almost every song. We often dance it during communion, while the gifts of bread and wine move through the crowd of communicants surrounding the altar table.

The short four-beat compass of these plain steps suits a wide variety of hymns in many meters (see table below). But used exclusively, they would prove monotonous. Congregations need something more varied and inventive (yet still easily learned and danced). Among a broad range of world traditions, we have found that Greek folk dances serve that purpose supremely well. The simplest are very ancient, some say as old as our Indo-European language family. Hellenistic mosaics suggest several were known to fourth-century and New Testament Christians and, perhaps, to Jesus himself. In our century, the Greek youth movement has standardized them, precisely in order to make them accessible to wider populations. Thanks to the wide diaspora of Greek immigrants and their hardy ethnic loyalty, many American cities boast Greek folk dance groups—often attached to Orthodox churches—who will gladly teach their fellow Americans how to join in. (The food at Greek festivals is a learners' bonus!) Many recordings and books supply simple explanations with footprint drawings. Folk dance clubs often boast libraries of such publications for inquirers to look through.

Though now commonly danced to eastern Mediterranean melodies in modal scales sprung from central Asia and India, Greek folk steps also transfer well to classical western hymn tunes, and distinctively suit congregational dance. Their repetitive rhythmic figures fit almost half the hymns in *The Hymnal 1982*. A few Greek steps do carry interpretive gestures; but most engage people through rhythmic repetition and variation, and so will serve widely different texts. In this way they parallel the secular couple dances which our worshipers know well. (The jitterbug, the tango, the latest rock dances all build on repetition and variation.) Thus Greek dances offer a folk vocabulary easily grafted onto American worship. They have a further virtue for our purpose: unlike other ethnic dances boasting vigorous vertical movements, these move sinuously, even sensuously sideways, providing the dancers a palpable feel of the whole community dancing together. Their sideways momentum also makes it easy to sing and dance at once, as each dancer can place one hand on a neighbor's shoulder, while the other hand holds a song sheet.

These Greek steps serve for our final dance at St. Gregory's, the carol ending each eucharist. After communion, and after collecting alms and food for the poor and setting these on the altar table, we circle the table teaching the dance step. Soon we are singing and dancing to the beat of drums, sistrums, and bells. The carol ends with a joyous Russian chant wishing "Many Years!" to those here celebrating birthdays and anniversaries; then coffee and cakes are laid out on the same altar table, and people continue the feast until all is gone.

Thus, the dance completes the service in a burst of (literally) touching community warmth. More than that, it gives everyone a vivid image of the world's hope and our true future, a mystical end to the mystical supper. Grasping this image for themselves, people overcome fears of awkwardness and take part as they may not have expected to. This author first introduced caroling as a once-yearly Easter event for spirited Yale chaplaincy students (including Gretchen Wolff Pritchard, another contributor to this volume). Later, the parishioners at St. Gregory's received it even more enthusiastically; the Sunday after Easter, they demanded to know why we weren't keeping the custom. So we have ever since, even at funerals—excepting only Good Friday, when everyone leaves church quietly to return for nearly an hour of caroling at the Easter Vigil. Moreover, caroling has proved remarkably inclusive, as most newcomers are willing to try it, and, trying it, most say they love it. A seminarian in an electric wheelchair learned to lead the dance during her fieldwork year with us, and other physically challenged visitors have joined in, too. Sometimes older people or little children will sit out one or both of the dances, as happens naturally in secular gatherings. But because our worship also offers many chances to sing without dancing, no one has complained of exclusion.

Many visitors have taken a love for caroling home with them, and some report they have planted it in receptive soil. Our workshops in nearby churches have produced mostly happy feedback, sometimes from the oldest parishioners present. We like to hope that other churches are developing congregational dances on their own. Despite a century or more of estrangement, the wedding of dance and worship is right and deep, and the friends of each have every cause to rejoice together. At this writing, St. Gregory's new church building is nearly completed. Our plans call for an open altar space, with plenty of dancing room around the table. Overhead—as quickly as we can pay for them!—icons of the saints will circle-dance with us, led by Christ the Lord of the Dance, and an inscription from those sayings preserved outside the gospels that scholars think may come authentically from Jesus himself:

> *"Whoever does not dance, does not know what is coming to pass."* (Acts of St. John)

Worship planners beginning caroling may find a few practical points useful. For simplicity's sake, and especially for the sake of enrolling newcomers to St. Gregory's, we carol to hymn tunes with regular lines of equal lengths. (Some tunes with a single short line can be danced in paired stanzas, provided the overall rhythm is clear. More irregular verse patterns may fit the *Tripudium* or *High Life* steps described above.) Of course we choose lyrics to match the readings or the liturgical moment. Then we fit steps to the number of dance beats per line, and the internal rhythm and tempo. Note that the number of dance beats results from the musical rhythm, not from the syllables or word accents. Hence the conventional metrical tune classification appendixed to most hymnals will not serve our purpose; instead we have begun compiling a table of danceable meters. Because these steps can dance fast or slow, following the text sense, the musical voice-leading, and everyone's need to take breath, each step will serve for various seasons and moods. We currently use six dance steps year round: their popular Greek names appear below, together with a few of the many hymns that dance well to them. *Sta Dyo* has proved easiest to learn, and can cover all eight- and four-beat hymns at first, while other steps are added as the people gain experience.

Table of Steps

Eight beats, or pairs of four beats per line:

Greek Step	Tune	*The Hymnal 1982*	
Sta Dyo	*Hyfrydol*	460	Alleluia! sing to Jesus . . .
		657	Love divine . . .
	In dulci jubilo	107	Good Christian friends, rejoice . . .
	Purpose	534	God is working his purpose out . . .
	St. Columba	645	The King of love . . .
	Torah Song	536	Open your ears . . .
Gaida	*Ballad*	673	The first one ever . . .
	Foundation	636	How firm a foundation . . .

Greek Step	Tune	*The Hymnal 1982*	
	Star in the East	118	Brightest and best . . .
	Simple Gifts	554	'Tis the gift to be simple . . .
Kalamatiano	*Easter Hymn*	207	Jesus Christ is risen today . . .
	Llanfair	214	Hail the day that sees him rise . . .
Syrto	*Aberystwyth*	640	Watchman, tell us of the night . . .
	Ellacombe	210	The day of resurrection . . .
	Erhalt uns	143	The glory of these forty days . . .
	Unser Herrscher	180	He is risen . . .
	Zeuch mich	286	Who are these like stars appearing . . .

Note that the *Tripudium* and *High Life* steps described above will fit any tune with four or eight dance beats per line—even tunes mixing lines of different lengths or tunes with three internal beats per measure.

Three or six beats per line:

Hasapiko	*Bourbon*	675	Take up your cross, the Savior said . . .
(Sta Tria)	*Bunessan*	8	Morning has broken . . .
	Kedron	10	New every morning is the love . . .
		163	Sunset to sunrise changes now . . .
	Love Unknown	458	My song is love unknown . . .

Five or ten beats per line:

Sweet Girl	*Gaudeamus pariter*	200	Come, ye faithful . . .
		237	Let us now our voices raise . . .

Some Thoughts about Worship in Congregations Numbering Fewer than Fifty

by Clayton L. Morris

Introduction

Small worshiping communities have unique qualities and needs. They require a style of worship which recognizes those particularities. All too often, however, small gatherings of worshipers are encouraged to accept the assumptions which are appropriate for worship planning in much larger communities.

It is with this notion in mind that suggestions are offered here for what might be called the typical small congregation. Defining small as a gathering of fewer than fifty people will seem to most Episcopalians to suggest a congregation smaller than is typical, but average attendance records from parochial reports indicate that these small gatherings represent 36 percent of congregations in the Episcopal Church.[25]

Size—the number of worshipers present at any given time—is not the only characteristic to be considered in conversations about worship in "small communities." Imagine, just for the fun of it, a eucharistic liturgy celebrated at the beach with four worshipers seated at a picnic table. A bottle of wine and crust of bread are produced from the picnic basket, and prayer books are opened. Then appear musical scores for the "Mass in Four Parts" by William Byrd. The use of a complex, polyphonic musical setting for the Gloria, Sanctus, and so forth seems improbable for a congregation of four about to begin an *al fresco* liturgy at the beginning of a picnic, unless, of course, the congregation happens to be a quartet of professionally-trained singers.

A small congregation of capable singers will respond to a different selection of music than will a gathering of worshipers with a different musical ability. A small congregation

[25]Attendance statistics from parochial reports in 1991 indicate the following average Sunday attendance in Episcopal congregations:

Average attendance size category	Number of congregations
0–25	1,420
26–50	1,261
51–150	2,986
151–350	1,438
350 and up	282

of worshipers who gather daily for worship will require a more diverse textual and musical repertoire than a congregation which meets once a week.

In short, liturgical planning is never a matter of blindly applying predetermined principles to a specific situation. Every gathering of Christians is unique. Every congregation must find its own liturgical style.

The intent of this essay is to consider some liturgical planning possibilities in reference to gatherings of small numbers of people. The small congregation to which this planning applies is a gathering attended by a typical sampling of worshipers (in contrast to the picnickers describer above). The liturgy envisioned as the result of these planning notions is one which understands—and even takes advantage of—the natural characteristics of this small congregation.

Sensitivity about Congregational Size

Why worry about numbers, anyway? Imagine a variety of social gatherings at which food is served. Four people gather intimately around a table. Conversation will generally include all four diners. A group of eight gathers around one table, but the sense of intimacy begins to fade. Perhaps two conversations or even three at a time begin to break the group into smaller enclaves, but a conversation of the whole is still manageable. The master of ceremonies at a banquet for a hundred guests has to ring a wine goblet to get the attention of the crowd in order to propose a toast. Yes, numbers matter. The assumptions informing liturgical planning change as the congregational size increases or decreases.

How Small is Small?

Perhaps this is the wrong question. It may be more accurate to wonder whether or not liturgical behavior matches the size of the community in which that behavior occurs. Behavior at a dinner party depends on the number of people present. If it is to be effective, liturgy must be planned and celebrated with a sensitivity to the number of people gathered.

In its architecture, the Episcopal Church demonstrates a fondness for Gothic space. In a few places, that fondness has provided a grand liturgical setting of great interest and importance. But in other places across the country, there are tiny churches, seating fewer than a hundred people, which exist as pitifully shrunken monuments to that architectural model. There is a nave, with a center aisle barely wide enough to accommodate a procession in single file. At the head of the aisle, past the altar rail, is a tiny sanctuary several steps above the nave, with seating for, perhaps, four persons. Although the square footage of such a space might be adequate for the actual number of regular worshipers, the configuration of that space—and the Gothic, even basilican, liturgical model that such a configuration enforces—tends to undercut and strangely "miniaturize" the worship that takes place there.

In its attention to music, the Episcopal Church has always been devoted to the great music of the choral tradition. Again, in some congregations, the fabulous musical heritage of Anglicanism can be heard magically performed Sunday by Sunday. But in many more congregations, vested choirs stand in one corner of the aforementioned shrunken mini-cathedral struggling to sing hymns in four parts and robbing the congregation of its musical leadership.

How small is small? A first principle in the design of liturgy is a simple one. In order to be effective, the spatial arrangement, choreography, music, vesture, and general ambience must be appropriate (useful) to the size of the congregation. When liturgical planners begin to design worship without a conscious understanding of what works best for the number of congregants with which they are working, the result likely will be artificial. If, on the other hand, the planners begin with an informed sensitivity to the effect of congregational size on liturgical form, the gathering will have an integrity of its own, and the result will be cohesive and life-giving.

Some Tools and Principles

The Episcopal Church is an increasingly diverse collection of communities. Diversity is apparent not only in terms of congregational size, but also in terms of the varieties of culture and language represented in the congregation. Thus, it will be impossible in this limited space to make suggestions for every conceivable circumstance. Instead, a series of questions will suggest approaches to problem-solving which will be effective in a variety of congregational circumstances.

Liturgical Space

Some small congregations worship in buildings too large for the number of people who gather. Some small congregations worship in a building not designed specifically for worship, maybe even in a private home. Some small congregations gather in borrowed or rented space. *Most* Episcopalians gather in seating arranged in "theater style," with worshipers in rows facing one end of a room where the celebrant and other leaders face the congregation.

Is this typical arrangement of furniture the best solution for a small gathering of people? Consider two alternatives:

A group of twenty-five people can comfortably gather in a single circle of chairs facing inward. A group of fifty can manage the same seating arrangement in double rows. The celebrant, readers, intercessors, and others in leadership roles can be seen and heard easily if they are seated in the circle with other worshipers.

Seats for the congregation might be placed in rows on the long axis of a rectangular space, with the seats facing the center of the room (sometimes called "collegiate style"). An ambo for reading and preaching can be placed at one end of the rectangle. The celebrant might be seated at the end opposite the ambo. Other leaders, intercessors, readers, or cantors might come to the ambo from their seats in the congregation.

Placement of an altar in arrangements like these might vary depending on the amount of space available. In the case of a building which is spacious—accommodating more people than gather week-by-week—it is possible to create two worship centers. The congregation can gather for the service of the word at one end of the nave, and move to stand around a table for the eucharistic meal at the other end. If the space is not large enough to allow the movement of the people from "word space" to "table space," the altar can be placed in the center of the gathering. Or, a simple table can be brought into the space at the time of the offertory.

A word about altars: When a congregation decides to experiment with space, it is useful to consider (reconsider) the size and shape of the altar to be used. A simple table will do. It should be more square than rectangular. If necessary, for the comfort of the presider, it can be raised two or three inches above the typical thirty-inch dining table height.

Small congregations are likely to be informal. People most likely know one another. Why should the liturgical space force people well acquainted with each other to avoid eye contact in the course of the liturgy? Does it make sense to create an auditorium-like space for a community whose lifestyle has a naturally communal quality?

Vesture

In general, Episcopalians have been led to believe that the rules about liturgical vesture were made by some authority external to the worshiping congregation, and it is expected that the local community will observe those rules. The congregation eager to develop a liturgical style suited to its particularities will be wise to question this authority. What does liturgical vesture mean? What do vestments accomplish in a liturgical gathering?

One could say much about the varied rationale for the use of vestments in worship, but in the context of small gatherings, two notions suggest a way of considering the question. In a large gathering, vestments identify people who have a leadership role in the liturgy. Thus, the alb might be used to identify persons filling those roles: celebrant, deacon, reader, intercessor, lay eucharistic minister, acolyte, for example. The priest and deacon would add to the alb the distinctive stole which is the symbol of their office. On "dress-up" occasions, chasubles, dalmatics, or copes might be added. Does this rationale for vesting apply to the small gathering of Christians, where the identity of the persons and the roles they play is not in question?

It is often noted that vestments lend an air of dignity to those so dressed and provide an appropriate level of anonymity to liturgical leadership. Both suggestions are probably true. Are these values which the small congregation should hold?

What about vestments for musicians? If there is a choir is the small worshiping community, for what purpose do they vest? Does the wearing of special clothes suggest special (i.e., separate) seating? If the congregation numbers twenty, and eight of those are members of the choir, should they be separated from the congregation for the entire liturgy? Why not assume that they take their places with their families and friends, moving from their places to gather as a choir when they are called upon to perform?

Selection of Vestments

Liturgical vestments should reflect the character of the congregation in which they will be worn. In small communities, where budget constraints often limit possibilities, taking advantage of locally-available materials and relying on local fabric artists will simultaneously save money and produce vesture of great authenticity. Unless a community has people capable of producing well-tailored garments, albs probably should be purchased commercially. Chasubles, stoles, and copes, on the other hand, are relatively easy to create for anyone with basic sewing skills.

The most important design features to consider in making vestments is shape and fabric. Let the shape of the vestment define it. Superimposing additional images, symbols, or topical references only adds confusion to the symbol of the garment itself. To create an interesting vestment, choose interesting fabric. While the four liturgical colors usually associated with the season of the church year help provide seasonal focus, there is nothing to prevent the vestment maker from varying the palette.

Movement

The liturgical procession, as we know it, is a device not particularly well-suited to small congregations. As lovely as it is to behold the vested ministers and the singers moving from narthex to sanctuary in flowing robes, led by cross, torches, and perhaps incense, this dance has no real function in a small congregational gathering.

The procession developed historically as a purposeful movement from one place to another, not merely as a means of transportation but with some liturgical or devotional significance. Contemporary practice preserves the procession in this sense when the gospel is processed into the midst of the people, or when clergy, candidate, and sponsors process to the font for baptism. The procession of vested ministers from one end of the church to the other does not derive from that tradition.

All too often, when the Sunday morning liturgy in a very small building begins with a procession, all present are aware of—and perhaps amused by—the fact that the vested party has gathered in the sacristy, which has a door leading directly to the sanctuary. Instead of moving into the liturgical space by the shortest route, the entire procession sneaks around the outside of the church in order to form a stately procession to the place from which they have just come.

How should the liturgy begin? In a congregation in which people are well acquainted, the gathering of worshipers is often a noisy event. People greet on another. The sight of a friend or neighbor reminds one of a message needing to be communicated. This is not an intrusion on the worship experience; indeed, it is a part of the gathering process. But it is probably a good thing to have a few minutes of quiet, serving as transition from acts of greeting to corporate prayer.

One possible replacement for the formal procession is the simple gesture of vested folks finding their places. Choristers, having vested and gathered their music, quietly take their places. The celebrant, likewise, enters the space quietly and takes the presider's chair. A moment will come when all are present. In the quiet of that moment, the celebrant stands and the liturgy begins. Another possibility represents a more active approach. The church has realized that the effective use of the broadened range of liturgical and musical resources requires explanation and rehearsal. Perhaps the musician(s) should preside over the *entire* gathering process, starting with the gathering of the worshipers "accompanied by" an informal rehearsal of some of the music to be used in the liturgy. Perhaps this rehearsal should take place around the piano or organ, and the entire congregation then processes to their seats when it is time to begin the service.

Again, an important planning consideration is to think about what works, not just in a practical sense, but also in the sense of what kind of liturgical gesture meets the needs of the small congregation.

Gesture

Dozens of books have been written on the subject of liturgical choreography. Several good selections are listed in the "For Further Reading" section. The question for those in positions of liturgical leadership in the small gathering is one of scale. Gestures intended to "read" across a huge space often look silly up close. Stylistic elements of liturgical choreography appropriate and necessary in a large building may be totally useless in a small space.

Text

It is difficult for people trained and nurtured in a liturgical tradition to celebrate the eucharist in a spirit of spontaneity. Consider, for example, the midweek eucharist on those occasions when one or two people arrive to join the waiting celebrant. Does the celebration adapt its style, on that occasion, to the number of people present? Do the three worshipers move to a table in another room, where they can be seated in close proximity? Does the formality of the Prayer Book discourse recognize the intimacy of the occasion? Or, does the celebration proceed as if the church were filled to capacity? And what about the celebrant who begins the Sunday service announcements with the habitual line of welcome to newcomers and visitors, even though the most cursory of glances at the twenty-two congregants present confirms that they are all long-time members of the congregation?

It is difficult to speak about editing the liturgical text of the eucharistic celebration, because the church is bound by canon to use texts approved by General Convention. But it is clearly the case that changes in the church's approved texts are made on the basis of the church's recognition of the need for change. As the church becomes increasingly aware that it exists as a collection of small congregations, it is important for those ministering in this context to explore how the prescribed text is to be made helpful to small gatherings.

Music

Anglicans are justifiably proud of their musical heritage. The tradition of choral and organ music in the Anglican tradition is rich and wonderfully expressive. But the application of this tradition to the small worshiping community is tenuous. For the most part, liturgical music in the Anglican tradition assumes an impressive array of music-making resources: a building with specific acoustical properties; a fine, custom-built organ; a well-trained, even professional, choir; an experienced organist-choir director, and a large music library.

Increasingly, one sees on the market machines designed to reproduce for the small congregation some semblance of this elaborate, Anglican musical ambience. One can purchase a device which, at the touch of a button, can "play" a hymn by mimicking a wide variety of musical instruments. Choose from pipe organ, piano, full orchestra, and so on. From time to time in parishes, one encounters recorded music as prelude to a eucharistic celebration.

The temptation to replicate the musical ambience of the cathedral is ever-present, especially when electronic wizardry abounds. But this is a temptation to be avoided at all costs. In the congregational setting, artificially-produced music is no more lively than are plastic flowers; neither is symbolic of life. From a strictly practical point of view, the use of "canned" music tends to imply a lack of confidence in the local indigenous musical talent—an unfortunate self-fulfilling prophecy which discourages musicians from coming forward with their time and skills.

Many will say that congregational singing is a thing of the past. While it is true that social gatherings are less likely to break out in song than was the case fifty or a hundred years ago, and, further, that our society no longer teaches its children to sing as a matter of course, the joy of congregational song must not be abandoned to the electronic craze which dominates the culture.

Perhaps it is the church's task to reintroduce informal, communal music-making to the culture. The congregation which is interested in promoting and preserving congregational music-making will find help from an increasing number of church musicians who are interested in this cause. The primary resource is always at hand. People bring their voices with them to church. What is needed is the opportunity to raise those voices in simple, accessible music and the leadership of at least one person who can "carry a tune."

Diocesan music commissions and the Standing Commission on Church Music have resources available to assist the local congregation in the development of a congregational music program. The Office of Liturgy and Music at the Episcopal Church Center can direct you to the people who can help you.

In Short . . .

Ideally, the liturgical planner will develop, in the process of making decisions about worship, a sense of what works well in the particular circumstance. Thoughtful considerations of the needs of the congregation will naturally lead to a liturgical plan which will be natural, nurturing, attractive, and expressive.

One way to keep one's bearings in the planning process, especially (but not exclusively) in the context of the small worshiping community, is to return time and again to visions of the dining room. Most folks have a natural sense of how best to offer hospitality to guests in their home. Those instincts about offering refreshment, comfort, and a sense of friendship to visitors serve well in liturgical planning. Notions that work well in the dining room are likely to find application, at least by analogy, in the eucharistic assembly.

Where Does the Church Go Wrong?

Why do small churches attempt to appropriate models and behaviors more suitable for large congregations? What is it that seduces the small congregation into a vision of grandeur which simply doesn't apply? Two responses come to mind.

While most Episcopal congregations are small- to medium-sized, many assume that the normative congregation is a medium- to large-sized community. We routinely assume that a worshiping congregation of Episcopalians has a fully equipped worship space (organ, etc.) and a complete staff (multiple clergy, professional musicians, choir, etc.). In fact, a growing number of congregations gather in a small room with simple furniture. There may be no musical instrument or paid staff to facilitate worship.

The real difficulty—which sits beneath the church's mistaken image of normative behavior—is the notion that authority is external to the life of the community. Anglicanism—and, thus, the Episcopal Church—is organized around assumptions of authority, but too often, what is assumed to represent authorized forms and styles are simply those which have become common and habitual.

Anglicans share a common understanding of worship which, more than anything else in the tradition, defines and identifies Anglicanism. There are two common misunderstandings of that tradition which continually confuse the church. While it is true that Anglicans are united in a common worship, it is not true that all Anglicans worship in identical style. While it is true that the tradition of liturgical use has united and does unite Anglicans, it cannot be said that Anglican liturgy is unchanging.

What Can Be Done?

How does the small community discover, develop, and use the resources available? The small worshiping community is a specific expression of life in the Episcopal Church. In much the same way that Native-American Episcopalians, Hispanic Episcopalians and Chinese Episcopalians are broadening and enriching the church's identity, the increasing awareness of the proliferation of small gatherings of Episcopalians is teaching the church new things about itself. Small communities struggling to live and worship in the context of baptism and eucharist need the freedom to discover liturgical ways of being that meet their needs. Just as cultural necessity has, from time to time, changed the shape and style of Anglican tradition, the discovery of authentic liturgical expression in small worshiping communities will add new richness to the tradition.

Those who plan liturgy need to pay more attention to the process of evaluating the unique needs of a particular community. Recognizing that standards and an appreciation of tradition are always important to Christians who worship in a sacramental context, planners need to apply more attention to the way in which those standards and traditions are adapted to the circumstances of the particular community. The challenge for the church in the next few years is to understand better the tradition which identifies it, so that processes of adaptation can offer the gift of that heritage to a wider range of communities and cultures. By looking carefully at what works in its liturgical gatherings, small worshiping communities can contribute significantly to that cause.

Dealing with Liturgy in Racially-Mixed Congregations

by Ernesto Medina

For the first time in the history of the Episcopal Church we find ourselves in a position to *admit* that we are a church which is not monocultural. It is important to note, however, that the Episcopal Church has been *non* monocultural for a long time. The reality of this situation in the life and prayers of the church has been too often overlooked. Worship communities find themselves confronted more and more with neighborhoods which are changing around them in dramatic ways. Clearly the gospel tells us to open the doors of worship to all, but change— especially the change of a worshiping community—is difficult and almost always painful. What follows is an examination of some of the liturgical issues which necessarily will challenge worshiping communities as they become more diverse. Then, moving from these particularities of worship, I will examine some of the larger implications of—and implications for—a church which is ready to admit that it just might look different than before.

Assumptions

Many of the conversations I have about liturgy result in misunderstandings. This is inevitable if we do not know one another's working assumptions as a particular vision of worship is being created. So, before sharing some practical tools for working with racially-diverse congregations, I will articulate my foundational assumptions.

First, although this paper deals with liturgy in racially-mixed congregations, the real issue for me is sharing the gospel as we enter the twenty-first century, regardless of the congregation's configuration. In other words, I really am attempting to answer the question, "What is the gospel of Jesus Christ telling us to *do* and *be* today?" It just so happens that inclusivity and reconciliation—on the local level or on national or international levels—are important elements of the challenge to the church today.

Second, our tradition considers that the liturgy and prayers provided in the Book of Common Prayer constitute our church's free gift to the rest of the world. The fact that the BCP is one of the few books not copyrighted is a concrete witness to this.

In addition, we understand that the Prayer Book is a dynamic document. It is a book which always is in need of revision (even when it first comes out). At the same time, we recognize that, with every change, with every revision, there is a cost, a sense of loss which will bring inevitable pain.

Yet the Book of Common Prayer is not the end-all of our tradition. In fact, it is my belief that the core of our Prayer Book tradition is not *the book* but the consistency with which every revision, beginning with Cranmer's, has attempted to make the prayers accessible to the people of God. It cannot be overstated that at the core of our Anglican tradition is the belief that worship is for the people of God—not for a selected elite! Many of the problems we as a church face today, with respect to the welcoming of people of different cultures and backgrounds and the attempt to do liturgy which might reflect the differences in culture, comes from the misunderstanding that liturgy essentially is fixed and that there is little need to change for other people. Many in our church believe that our liturgy is valuable but are only willing to offer it to the world with strings attached. This is contrary to our tradition.

Third, it is the responsibility of the gathered local community to provide a welcoming place of worship. The community has to decide whether they believe the gospel calls them to share the good news with people who are like them, a little different, or very different. It is not appropriate for a community to welcome the world only to impose its understanding of "proper" worship upon those who respond to the invitation. Especially if there is no willingness to change or risk. Too many worship communities like to proclaim the gospel so long as it is convenient or not a threat to their power. Too many worship communities want to welcome others, but with the condition that those coming in must conform to the status quo. When these things happen, barriers become well established and block the ability to offer viable liturgy in diverse communities.

Fourth, "multicultural" liturgy (many terms may be substituted) is a term too often used to protect the self-interest of a few. It is a phrase often used to describe what "they" do down the street or what might be done at the large diocesan events ("We, of course, do *liturgy* in our church"). Whatever phrase is used, my hope is that liturgy will be, in and of itself, a living expression of the gospel of Jesus Christ. The result, necessarily, would be liturgy that is "multicultural."

"Multicultural" or "inclusive" liturgy does not mean having two African Americans sitting in the pews, or asking someone to read the second reading in Spanish. Nor does it count if everyone gets to sing music that no one can pronounce! What occurs too often, when we attempt to include everyone in superficial ways in the liturgy, is that the designers search for the lowest common denominator. This will not work! In designing liturgies which are inclusive, we must begin looking for the *highest* common denominator (more on this later).

Finally, viable liturgy in racially-mixed congregations *is* possible. There are some in the church who do not share this belief. Multicultural liturgy should not be the goal for all congregations. There are many communities which need not be multicultural and, in fact, would do a better job of responding to the gospel by reflecting their unique cultural roots and traditions. It ultimately comes down to whether or not a community is willing to be open, trusting and vulnerable, and whether or not it considers its worship an unconditional gift to the world.

These are the assumptions I use in dealing with liturgy in racially-mixed congregations:

- At the heart of the design of any liturgy is our dealing with the question "What is the gospel of Jesus Christ telling us to do and be today?"
- The Book of Common Prayers serves as an icon of our Anglican/Episcopal identity, not in the words and liturgy per se but in its consistent intent to be a dynamic document assisting the people of God to worship.
- The gathered worshiping community has the primary responsibility to welcome others into the church. If a community wants to be welcoming, it must also be willing to change.
- Multicultural liturgy is *not* having someone read the second reading in Spanish, et al.
- Liturgy *is* viable with people of diverse backgrounds and experiences. It need not be the goal for all communities within the church.

Practical

Letting Go of Some of Our Assumptions

I begin with an extreme statement and an extreme example. We must let go of the many ways we live out our assumptions about what might be Anglican or Episcopal. It is true, for example, that we are a eucharistic people. This is a foundational statement of our tradition. We live this out by saying "The Holy Eucharist [is] the principal act of Christian worship on the Lord's Day. . . . " We assume that bread and wine are essential to the eucharistic feast. It is part of our Prayer Book. It is our usual practice. Yet it is my contention that one need not have bread and wine to be eucharistic or to have eucharistic celebrations. If, for example, you and five of your closest church friends found yourself marooned on Mars with neither bread nor wine, no doubt your new community would (and should) find a different way to celebrate the eucharist and be eucharistic.

I am by no means suggesting we give up the bread and wine, at least not in most places. But we must keep in mind what are the true foundations of our traditions and be open to the very different variations that may spring from these foundations.

There are other examples of things we might consider "letting go." We are a people of common prayer. This does not necessarily mean that we are a people who must pray in the same language, move our hands in the same way, or even use the same book. We are a people who come to church. This does not mean that the church has to be built pointing in the proper direction, that seats or pews have to be facing a certain way, that choirs are up in front or choirs are in the back. It does not mean that vestments must follow a particular design or pattern, or even that the liturgy must follow a particular order.

The point I am trying to make is that we spend too much time trying to force others into our particular forms of worship and, further, that we spend relatively little time exploring what the Holy Spirit might be saying to us about the true gospel foundations of our worship forms.

I remember going to a church in the South Side of Chicago where they seemed to break every liturgical rule in the book. It was Lent and there were "Alleluia" banners hung all around the walls. Church started fifteen minutes late. The choir danced around the altar, using hand-held microphones, and taped music, of all things. There was a seven-song entrance rite. By the fourth song, we were all dancing around the altar and aisles. Songs ended, the offertory sentence was given, and a little boy took an empty basket up to the altar and turned around. The entire congregation came forward and placed their gifts in the basket. Bread and wine were offered. Eucharistic Prayer A. Following communion, we heard the lessons, "broke open" the readings in the sermon, prayed some more, and ended the liturgy. The peculiar thing about the entire experience was that it was one of the most Anglican services I have ever experienced. Things were not in the order I expected, but, without a doubt, I knew we, as a community, had shared common prayer and been eucharistic. There was no doubt in my mind that I had been in an Episcopal church.

If we are willing to do liturgy with a variety of people, we have to be open to the possibility that any worshipful action may be done in a better manner. If we are to provide liturgy for a variety of people, the community must be willing to let go and explore different ways of worshiping God. If a community is not willing to do this, especially those who hold the power, empowering worship (of any kind) will not occur.

Willing to See God Through the Eyes of Another

Much excitement has been generated in the American church as we have playfully prayed the bilingual/bicultural liturgies of the New Zealand Prayer Book. Many people have had their perception of God nurtured further by being able to experience God through the eyes of the people of New Zealand, people culturally very different from ourselves. I am sure there are exceptions, but, as a rule, the New Zealand Book of Common Prayer has fed the American church. As different as this book may be from own Prayer Book, most of us who have used it see it as a very Anglican book, rooted in a common heritage. Even so, can we Episcopalians even imagine a discussion at our next General Convention of having a bilingual/bicultural Prayer Book? The resulting fights and battles would be truly frightening! On the other hand, the possibility of finally embracing the cultures found within our own church with the same openness with which we embraced the New Zealand book fills me with the satisfaction of the gospel.

The process is quite simple. The community's members are curious about others' perceptions of God; they observe, and they ask questions. Everyone has the opportunity to share experiences of the divine. The act of hearing these stories nurtures everybody's spiritual lives. The community continues to be nurtured as they reflect on the common threads—and the uncommon threads—in the stories they have exchanged.

I am amazed at how this simple process transforms communities. The result is a pretty solid foundation for a congregation preparing to do liturgy with persons of diverse backgrounds and experiences. Trust and vulnerability are established and people can be empowered to make the statement we all want to make: "Help me to see God." Liturgy is the response.

It is important to point out that words will not be the only way to communicate one's own experience of God or to discover someone else's experience of God. If one is open, one must expect surprises. Possibilities of communication include—but are not limited to—listening to the cadence or tones of words; watching the gesture of a hand or the movement of the eyes. At some point, there is a recognition that God is present in the moment, and lives are linked.

Mutuality is critical. The willingness to share must be equal to one's willingness to receive. It is a problem when a community invites others into their group (with good intentions) because they have a great experience of God and want to share it with the world, but then forget to listen to those invited.

A caution. As we offer our gift of God to others through our stories, it is important to realize that all will change, including perhaps our own story. What we do with gifts is strange sometimes. We like to give them out and then expect the receiver to keep them just the way they were given. In the giving and receiving of gifts, we must be willing to allow the gifts to be broken open so that God's grace may shine through.

Telling the Story of Jesus

One of the primary responsibilities of the Christian community is to tell the story of Jesus Christ. Although this might seem like a point made in Christian Education 101, it is a point too often forgotten in churches. "Tell the story of Jesus, and they will come," some will say.

Emphasis needs to be put on the simple telling of the story and not in exercises which attempt to explain the story. This is especially true when a lot of explanation comes *without* even *telling* the story!

There is the basic, sit-in-a-circle-and-read-from-the-Bible method. This is semi-effective. But a community who also struggles to find different ways, different methods for hearing and experiencing the story of Jesus will find itself open to God showing it how to do multicultural liturgy. With this we begin to entertain the notion of the *high common denominator*.

In multilingual communities, the question we are called to struggle with is, "How can we effectively tell a story so that all might understand?" Assumptions need to be left behind. Maybe the way to hear/experience the story is not to have one person recite a passage. Maybe it is one person non-verbally communicating the story. Perhaps it is several persons together, engaging their voices in different languages, an act which in and of itself helps tell the story. The sky is the limit.

The community may find that it only need to tell the story in several languages, one after another. This is OK, for at least the entire community is dealing with the issue and no one particular group will feel left out of the process. I would, however, maintain that the more a community creatively engages in telling the story, the better prepared for liturgy it will be.

When it comes to "breaking open" the word, the community may find it interesting to consider the possibility that "sermon" might no longer mean the priest speaking to the masses from the pulpit. Can we consider the loss of rhetorical sermons? Can clergy realize that the people might have effective tools to break open the word for each other? The answer I propose is "Yes!" Simply stated, the community should be given the primary responsibility of telling the story of Jesus.

The principal points are these. We need to tell the story of Jesus. We need to wrestle as a community to find ways in which all can experience the story. It is through wrestling with the issue that the word will be broken open like never before, and people will find themselves linked together at a very deep level. If one concentrates on the telling of the story of Jesus only, the sharing of our own faith stories will naturally follow. If a community figures out how to tell the story for all, then it figures out how to break open the story for all as well.

Children: One of the Highest Common Denominators

The Office of Children's Ministries of the Episcopal Church Center has coordinated a discussion called the "Treasure Kids" project over the last five years. This project which was led by educators and advocates from over a dozen dioceses has struggled with the issue of the care and nurture of children by our church. The result of their work can be summarized in a document called "A Children's Charter for the Church." Earlier I stated that multicultural liturgy will not work well if we go for the lowest common denominator but can do well if we struggle with finding the highest common denominator among the people gathered. The "Children's Charter" is a document which articulates how to struggle for the highest common denominator.

I would like to point out two specific points from the "Charter" and then suggest how they may be used in the development of multicultural liturgies:

- The church is called to include children, in fulfillment of the baptismal covenant, as members and full participants in the eucharistic community and in the church's common life of prayer, witness, and service.
- The church is called to appreciate children's abilities and readiness to represent Christ and his church, to bear witness to him wherever they may be, and according to gifts given them, to carry on Christ's work of reconciliation in the world, and to take their place in the life, worship, and governance of the church.

I maintain that the "Children's Charter" is in reality a charter for everyone, that anywhere the charter mentions "child" or "children," one can easily replace it with "person" or "persons." What the charter allows one to do is to see children as the opportunity to do the ministry of the church. Everyone wins in this model!

Children allow a community to wrestle safely with the issues of inclusion, because they are not as threatening as adults. Some might say, "We can do *that* for the children." In the nurture and caring for children, communities are then able to care for and nurture the rest of the community.

Imagine, if you will, a community which will take the two points from the charter, focusing all its attention on how to integrate the children fully into the complete life of the church. No longer do the cultural differences appear as barriers, but as opportunities for the sharing of stories and of faith. The seeds are then well planted for designing liturgies for multicultural congregations. I would dare say that a monocultural community that honestly struggles with how to integrate children into the life of the church will, in fact, establish a welcoming place for persons of many backgrounds and all ages. This is perhaps a new way of experiencing the passage, "a little child shall lead them" (Isaiah 11:6).

Most places are fairly comfortable with wanting to share their faith, traditions, and spirituality with the children. The charter invites communities to deal with the question, "What structures will be developed so that the children can share their spirituality and their other gifts with the larger church?" Inviting a congregation to deal with this question will result in new ways of telling the story of Jesus (i.e., learning to see God through the eyes of another), and will actually give communities the courage to let go of many assumptions.

Rites of Passage

Here is another lesson we can learn from having children integrated into our worship lives—a lesson we can then reapply in our ministry to adults: the children among us are a constant reminder of the rites of passage in our lives; after all, children grow up, leave our worship communities, and (if we are lucky) come back again. We may confront these rites of passage somewhat passively, but at least we confront them.

Multicultural communities are well served by *proactive* rites of passage. Since they do not really exist in our church, except in rare situations, we will have to look at models provided by other cultures. This step—looking at other cultures—is important as we deal with developing viable liturgies. Communities will be able to discover common ground as they find ways to give thanks for the life of a person as well as that person's transition into adulthood with all its gifts and privileges.

A possible result of developing rites of passage for our youth and children is the acknowledgment that adults also experience change or transitions. The church can find ways to celebrate them and pray them along their journey. Again, more common experiences for the community.

Using the Order for Eucharist

"An Order for Celebrating the Holy Eucharist" (BCP, page 400) provides a most helpful tool for communities wanting to develop inclusive liturgies. This order of service is an excellent starting point, for it releases a community from a liturgical language found in our current eucharistic rites. Order of service language found in most church bulletins (e.g., The Opening Acclamation; The Collect of the Day; Gradual Hymn; The Sermon; The Prayers of the People; Eucharistic Prayer A; Fraction Anthem; Post-Communion Prayer) is not helpful, because this language comes associated with a certain way of performing liturgical actions.

Here is an outline of "An Order for Celebrating the Holy Eucharist":

The Priest and People
Gather in the Lord's Name
Proclaim and Respond to the Word of God
Pray for the World and the Church
Exchange the Peace
Prepare the Table
Make Eucharist
Break the Bread
Share the Gifts of God

This form allows for a fresh look at how a community gathers and will be a eucharistic people. It is easier to talk about how best to "Gather in the Lord's Name" than to do inclusive liturgy by trying to find the correct collect of the day. The outline suggests we might consider different ways of proclaiming and responding to the word of God: readings, song, talk, dance, other art forms. This is very different than the common litany: one person reads from the Old Testament, all say the psalm, another person reads from the New Testament, all sing a song, the gospel is read. New language gives us new tools. If not everyone understands the same language, we are now given permission to find a new way to tell the story.

The rest of the outline can be dealt with in a similar way. First, ask, "How do we do this liturgical action now?" Second, ask, "What do the new words or phrases found in the outline really allow us to do?" The fact that some of the points found under the bold headings are blank is permission for freedom! Third, dream together.

Please note the first rubric found in the outline: "This rite requires careful preparation by the Priest and other participants." If nothing else is communicated in this paper, it is my hope that it be understood that liturgy must be the work of the people, and that planning should not occur with a priest and perhaps a selected few, but that the greater community must all wrestle with what it is to pray together.

Music, Space, and Movement

The selection of music and how to incorporate the music into liturgy is certainly a big challenge for any community. Let me begin this discussion by saying that most churches do not comprehend the depth of musical resources available. It is my experience that most congregations in the Episcopal Church are lucky if they know ten percent of the music in *The Hymnal 1982* (and that ten percent is made up mainly of the old standards).

For multicultural liturgy to be developed, entire congregations (not just the choir) are going to have to learn some new songs. The people in the congregations also are going to have to understand that they have permission to sing with some pep! If children are helping to guide a community as suggested above, this will be a lot easier. I want to say also that one does not have to sing "kids'" songs to be inclusive of children!

The Taizé community provides rich musical resources for communities that speak different languages, but these will not be enough for most congregations because the contemplative nature of this music will need to be balanced by other styles of music. It is important, however, to see what it is about Taizé music that makes it effective. First, is its repetitive design, one or two phrases of music sung by all with a cantor or cantors leading in different languages. Second, one need not be a trained musician to sing the music. Third, various options of instrumentation are available, and permission is given to use whatever musical tools are at hand. Finally, while the music is simple, it is not simplistic.

Using these criteria should be helpful for finding other viable music for liturgy in various resources. Whatever the music found, the congregation is going to have to be introduced to it and have good opportunity to practice. If the words are in a language foreign to some, others in the community (not just the musician) should be given the opportunity to teach the beauty of their own language. Not many things hurt the ear more than hearing your own language trashed!

It certainly is possible for congregations to arrange or compose some of their own music and probably important for more than one person to be allowed to provide instrumentation for the singing.

I think it obvious that, if a community seriously considers some of the methods I have presented, the liturgical space will need to be changed. In addition, inclusive liturgy is going to have to include the ability to move around and to physically live out our faith in church in a less passive manner. The truth is that most church architecture is not helpful for communities made up of *one* culture, much less for those made up of *many*. Our churches are designed essentially to convey that the priest has all the answers and that the people should sit down and listen. This certainly would not be consistent with what I am trying to communicate.

Communities are going to have to look at the space and resources they have and decide how best to change it for better expressions of their prayers. If a group of people come up with a great way to tell the story of Jesus, they need to ask next, "What kind of space do we need?"

On the facing page is a picture of what I might consider "a great space for liturgy." The purpose of sharing it is not to tell you how to change your space, but to begin the process of generating ideas of space and movement for your own situation.

Looking Toward the Future

It is my hope that very soon the discussion of how to do multicultural liturgy might end, not because we give up on the whole idea, but because we figure out how to do it and find ourselves moving toward some other issue. Just like the time we figured out we could pray in English!

As I end this discussion on multicultural liturgy or rather the liturgy of the church, let me map out a possibility for the future. I find it to be a hopeful picture. But first let us go back in time . . .

Centuries ago, the church was run by the few educated of the world. Information was contained within the walls of libraries found in monasteries. The people, at the same time, searched for God. Then came the great invention of the printing press, and, with this great invention, information became more accessible to the people, rather than the selected few. The people continued their search for God, but, now armed with this new technological tool, they found the quest a bit easier. Within our tradition, the Prayer Book was born, a radical move from the past. Worship was of the people, and technology was used to the best advantage.

We have been a fairly faithful people when it comes to remembering our tradition. Every revision of the Prayer Book is a continuation of making worship easier and more reflective of the needs of the community. In fact, the church became very

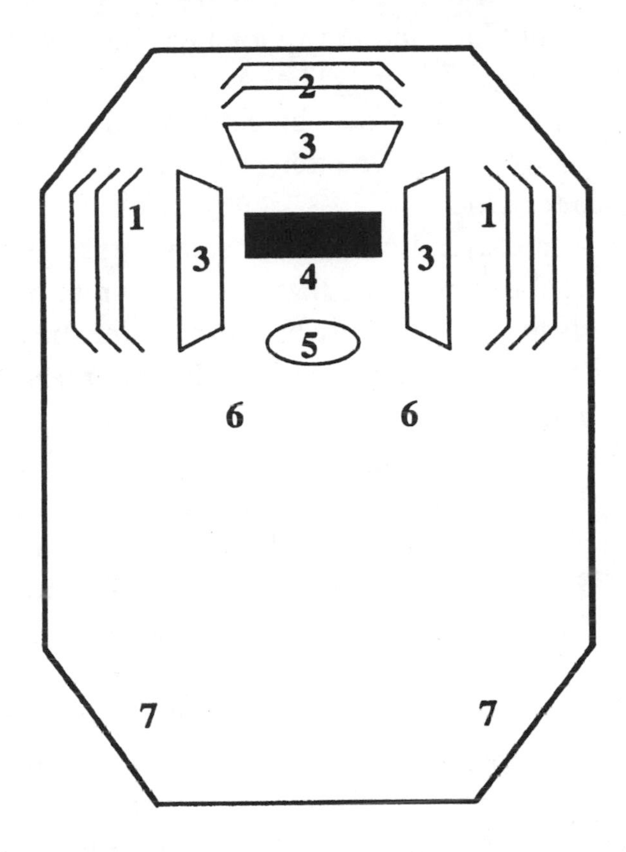

The following is a description of the liturgical space given above:

#1 This is where the congregation sits when they need to be seated. This position allows them to be close to the altar and also allows them to be facing other members of the congregation.

#2 This section is where the choir is placed. This placement allows the choir to be part of the congregation, while still allowing it to lead in the ministry of singing.

#3 This area is for the children to sit. It is an area with very good and comfortable carpet. This placement allows the children to be active members of the worshiping community. For those who are concerned by the behavior of the children, let me say that it is the responsibility of the gathered community to make the service interesting enough for the children. It is not their fault if the liturgy is boring! One may consider placing some rocking chairs here so that adults may hold a baby in this area of honor.

#4 The altar is central to the worshiping community. The presider may consider standing facing the choir for the eucharistic prayer.

#5 The font is placed in a position which reinforces our theology of baptism.

#6 This is open space to be used for the liturgy of the word. It is an open area to allow for the greatest flexibilities.

#7 The entrance to the church is here so that anyone entering the space sees clear passage to the altar.

This, of course, is only one suggestion and not meant to be the answer for all. Each community must wrestle with how best to proclaim its life with the gospel of Jesus Christ.

good at developing a Book of Common Prayer for a people who shared common roots.

But lately, the community has changed. The community has changed for a variety of reasons, one of which is the fact that the church went out and evangelized (in some places, with some pretty good results). One thing that hasn't changed is that the people, all the people, still search for God.

The last revision of our Prayer Book (1979) shows attempts not only at making liturgy more accessible, but also recognizing that the community had begun to change in ways different than ever before. We literally had reached for the stars during the 1960s and 1970s and had for the first time seen a world without borders. It is no accident that Eucharistic Prayer C is in our current book.

We are at the point where, as a church, we can admit to ourselves that we have grown past being a monocultural community. Assuming the best, we will be consistent with our tradition and once again move towards good and viable liturgy for the gathered community. But how? This is the question which faces all of us. For now it looks again like a selected few control the information, but all of us still search for God.

It appears as if history is repeating itself. With our new computer technology, the speed of information, the amount of information available at an inexpensive price and the availability of this technology, we find ourselves in an historic period of technological breakthrough. Many, I'm sure, are saying, "But computers are not cheap and certainly not available to all." My response is, "Look at how things were twenty years ago and compare that to now; now, look ahead twenty years and imagine, given the current rate of change, where we might be. In the grand scheme of things, twenty years is nothing."

Four realities come together. First, the church no longer is made up of one culture or language. Second, we have new technology that economically frees us from having to put our prayer life into a book that is only 1,000 pages long. Third, people are still searching for God. And fourth, we are people of God, Anglican in our tradition, and always moving to make worship accessible for the community. If we are consistent with our tradition, the result will be viable worship for our new community!

Given the current technology, it is possible to have a CD-ROM which contains not only the liturgy of our current Prayer Book, but liturgies from around the world and, in fact, liturgies from communities within our church that have already struggled with inclusive liturgy. This is all part of being willing to see God through the eyes of another.

I do not suggest that we should put computers in the pews at this time (we'll probably have the computers on our watches in twenty years, anyway), but I am suggesting that, by taking advantage of our current technology, we can see more clearly the many forms and rhythms of prayer of the many different people who worship within our own tradition. Some of these forms may be very cultural-specific. Other may reflect many cultural and worship traditions. But all can be understood as being consistent with the Anglican tradition.

We are at the most exciting time in history. The various new realities we face challenge us, bringing both pain and joy. Some things will have to die in order to make way for the birth (or rebirth) of others. We are very different than we were even a few decades ago. The development of liturgy for multicultural congregations is part of the journey we all walk together in order to more fully proclaim the gospel of Jesus Christ. Underneath it, of course, are the simple truths: that we need to tell the story of Jesus; that we need to listen to one another. Sin often gets in the way. We are also a people of hope, a people who cry, "Let the people pray."

Consistent with our Anglican identity, we now prepare to embrace a multicultural community, technology, and heritage in order to prepare to be the church for the future.

Planning Strategies

How to Form a Parish Worship Committee

by Juan Oliver

A parish worship committee may be appointed by the rector or vicar, meeting regularly to consider, advise, and suggest liturgical decisions to be made by him or her. Thus, the role of the committee is advisory.

A good worship committee is made up of persons who are deeply interested in liturgy, willing to learn more, and eager to work at it. Often the committee will be considering new ways of doing things. It is essential that the members be comfortable with experimentation and change, while holding each other accountable to the essentials of the liturgy.

Two types of members need to be included: people who, by the nature of their work, are involved in the preparations for liturgies, and people from a variety of ages and walks of life, who approach liturgy with no particular area of responsibility.

Among the first group may be listed *ex officio* members such as the rector, vicar, or priest in charge, deacon(s) and other assisting clergy, music and choir director(s), altar guild chairperson or sacristan, usher coordinator, acolyte coordinator, and reader coordinator.

A Healthy Liturgy Committee

Open communication is encouraged. Every member can lay out personal likes and dislikes, then try to transcend them by working towards what is appropriate for the congregation.

The expertise of specific people, such as the preachers, musicians, sacristan, is respected. Committee members delegate to each other, trusting each other's ability to work responsibly.

Micro-management is discouraged. The committee exists to map out broad areas of liturgical planning such as the nature and "feel" of Lent or Easter. Specific decisions, such as hymn choices, are entrusted to qualified persons. Let the music director, under the rector's supervision, select hymns. Let the altar guild select flowers; but do not leave overall decisions to a single group (for example, the decisions to celebrate Easter for a full fifty days). These broad decisions need to be made in the worship committee and shared by the members.

Plan *seasons*, not individual liturgies. A convenient set of planning seasons might be: Advent and Christmastide; Epiphany; Lent; Easter; early Pentecost; mid-Pentecost; late Pentecost. Each of these will last between six and eight weeks. Preparing two to three months ahead is not too soon.

Concerning each season, the committee might ask:

- How does the season function within the rhythm of the church year? Is the season preparing us for something? Is it celebrating and "digesting" a previous feast? Is it "ordinary time" ("green" seasons)?
- What is the tone of the season? Sober? Watchful? Deliriously festive?
- Look at the lectionary for the season in question, gospels first. What are the central images in this series of readings? How do these images throw light on the central symbolic actions of Christians: gathering morning and evening to celebrate the beginning and end of the day; listening to and sharing the word of God; washing and anointing new members; praying for the world and for the church; sharing a meal at the table of the reign of God.
- What spatial changes might be made to effect a particular atmosphere within the church building for this season?
- How may the many options presented within the Book of Common Prayer (the rubrics of Rite Two, for example, present over fifty options) be chosen to create a seasonal pattern of worship which will enhance the congregation's sense of moving through time while reassuring their need for continuity and stability?
- How will these options be exercised within the structure of the rite, so as to not overwhelm the essentials?

For example, a worship committee might suggest beginning the liturgy in Lent with the ministers already in prayer at their seats as the people arrive. Then would follow an acclamation, a short hymn or canticle, and the collect of the day—a bare bones approach which calls for the people to arrive on time if they are to catch the first lesson!

During Easter, the same committee might suggest gathering outside if weather permits, entering the church together in a festive procession while singing a baptismal Easter hymn and sprinkling the people with water, concluding when all are in their places, with the collect.

Through its imaginative planning work, the worship committee helps the congregation to unpack, season by season, the myriad meanings and attitudes found in the Christian kernel of meaning: the Easter mystery. This ongoing, ever-changing liturgical kaleidoscope presents, better than any sermon, the mystery of Christ among us, eternal yet ever new.

For more pointers on developing a worship committee for your parish see the brochure, *The Parish Worship Committee,* published by the Associated Parishes, P.O. Box 123003, Fort Worth, TX 76121-3003, PH: 817-535-1870.

You might also consult Thomas Baker and Francis Ferrone, *Liturgy Committee Basics: A No-nonsense Guide,* Washington, D.C.: The Pastoral Press, 1985; a detailed review of the tasks and pitfalls of working with a liturgy committee, written from a Roman Catholic point of view, but very applicable to Episcopal congregations as well.

How to Create a Worship Workshop in Three Sessions

by Joseph P. Russell

If we are to involve a variety of people in planning the worship of the congregation in the way envisioned by some of the articles in this book, people need training in the tradition, theology, and practice of worship in the Episcopal Church. The design for such a training program might look something like this:

Purpose: To explore the Book of Common Prayer and worship traditions as they are practiced in the Episcopal Church, in order to develop planning skills.

Session One: Prayer Book Skills

In this session participants are led through the pertinent sections of the Prayer Book that they need to understand for the planning task. The theology, tradition, and structure of the various rites are shared. Participants are encouraged to talk about their own experiences with the rites under study. If the participants are going to plan the liturgy for a particular season, the traditions of that season are explored along with the customary practices of the congregation.

Session Two: Bible Skills

Participants are given appropriate academic tools and resources so that they can appreciate the literature and theology of the Bible. They practice a variety of approaches to Bible study. Attention is given to the lectionary so that participants can understand the principles of designing worship within the structure of the lectionary.

Session Three: Putting the Liturgy Together

Participants look at the choices that can be made in designing worship in accordance with the rubrics of the Prayer Book. The following worksheet may help to clarify the options available to the planning team. If the worship is not a principal Sunday celebration of the eucharist, consider the flexibility afforded by "An Order for Celebrating the Holy Eucharist" (BCP, pages 400–405).

Planning for the Eucharist

How shall we gather in the Lord's name?

The entrance can be embellished with entrance hymn and procession, salutation, Collect for Purity, Song of Praise ("Glory to God in the Highest" or alternatives, rubrics pages 324, 356, 406), and Collect of the Day. A simpler option is to let the Song of Praise after the salutation serve as an opening hymn and move directly from salutation to Song of Praise to the Collect of the Day. Other variations to fit the occasion are possible.

How shall we proclaim and respond to the word of God?

The rubrics: *One or two Lessons, as appointed are read. . . . Silence may follow. A Psalm, hymn, or anthem may follow each Reading.* The gospel is read.

How shall we pray for the world and the church?

Note the rubric: *Any of the forms which follow may be used. Adaptations or insertions suitable to the occasion may be made.* Intercessions can be written or adapted by the planning team that reflect the biblical texts and the direct concerns of the congregation.

The confession of sin may be incorporated into the intercessions, may follow the forms on pages 331 or 360, or it may be omitted.

When shall we exchange the peace?

At what point in the service will "The Peace" have its greatest impact?

How shall we prepare the table?

Note that any sentence of scripture can be used as an "Offertory Sentence," if one is used. A hymn, psalm, or anthem may be sung.

How shall we make eucharist?

Two forms of eucharistic prayers are offered in Rite One, four in Rite Two. Choose the prayer that reflects the biblical texts and the occasion. When "An Order for Celebrating the Holy Eucharist" is used, the prayer may be written for the specific occasion.

How shall we break the bread?

Note the rubric: *In place of, or in addition to ["Christ our Passover"], some other suitable anthem may be used.* (See *The Hymnal 1982*, S151 through S172.)

How shall we share the gifts?

How shall we "go forth into the world?"

Hymn before or after the postcommunion prayer?

The blessing (optional), BCP, page 366.

See *The Book of Occasional Services*, for seasonal blessings.

See *Supplemental Liturgical Materials* for additional forms of blessing.

How to Review and Evaluate a Congregation's Worship Program

by Joseph Robinson

How can congregations evaluate the way they are designing and experiencing liturgical worship? In this article my purpose is not so much to answer as to wonder, not so much to correct as to improve, not so much to ensure that we are doing liturgy right as to illuminate the things that help us to do liturgy well. I will not suggest ways to fix the offertory or the entrance rite in your particular situation; rather, I suggest a look at the whole of the congregation's liturgical life. My hope is to help you see the meaning of how you worship together and what it is that is good and joyful and feeding about the time you spend in worship together.

I will assume that you who use this article in evaluating your liturgies will have a working knowledge of the Book of Common Prayer, including an understanding of the rubrics and conventions that guide the way we use that document when we are at prayer.

Prose or Poetry, the Modern Dilemma[27]

Twentieth-century Americans are such a hurried, harried lot that we often see ourselves as people who have no time for the poetic, the intuitive, the not-quite-so-direct approaches to worship that seem to me to provide the very glue that holds common prayer together. Like Sergeant Joe Friday of "Dragnet" fame, we are interested in "just the facts, ma'am." And each of us knows some person who can recite all the "dos" and "don'ts" of the eucharistic rubrics, who can dissect a service down to the smallest phrase of a collect, who can trace for us the historic lineage of a piece of service music, but who, when standing at the altar, appears to be rehearsing an endless list of details that seem related only in that they happen in the same place and at roughly the same time. This is what happens when we look at the eucharist in prosaic terms, as the sum of so many diagrammable sentences to be done in the right order under a certain set of conditions.

To look at the eucharist in poetic terms, in terms that seek a unity of time, place, and

[27]Note that "poetry" and "prose" are used throughout this article to refer, not to those literary forms in the strictest sense (whatever the "strict" sense of "poetry" and "prose" may be), but to our associations with those words (e.g., poetry = non-linear, intuitive; prose = linear, rational).

person, and a unity of all of that with God, is to experience the eucharist as dance, as our own God-given ability to move through space and time with balance and dignity and purpose; to make meaning out of the reading of lessons, the singing of hymns, the praying of prayers, and the breaking of bread. This is the eucharistic experience to which I am drawn, not a diagrammable so much as a transcendent experience in which I can lose myself in the greatness of God; where lives are changed and relationships strengthened and covenants begun. This is the eucharistic experience that I want to help you build by looking at a few of the ingredients available, and by asking a few questions about the finished product.

How the Eucharist Shapes My Life

There is a basic shape to my life that is supplied by my being a person of eucharistic practice. I want to share it with you here because you have a shape to your own life that may be similar. For practical purposes let us use the time frame of a week. The hinge pin for me is at a midpoint in the eucharist on the first day of that week—the little Easter that I celebrate each Sunday by gathering to be fed with other Christians. That midpoint of the service is called "The Offertory." It happens after I have gathered with my faith community; after I have heard the collect of the day and the lessons appointed for that day. It happens after I have sung a few hymns which support the lessons and themes of the day and after I have listened to a sermon which ties those themes and ideas up for me, reminding me that I am God's and not my own, and pointing me toward some action in the world. It happens after I have recited the eucharistic creed of the church, remembering those things that "We Believe," and after I have prayed for the church and the world, including prayers for the forgiveness of my own sins. It happens after I have been forgiven.

I sit down with the rest of the congregation, and we place symbols of our lives into a plate that is passed among us. A few generations ago we would have placed the produce of our land in the plate, but our culture runs on money, so that is what we bring as the symbol of our life and labor. This money, accompanied by symbolic gifts of bread and wine, is taken by members of the congregation to the altar. At the altar, the gifts are set on the table and the eucharist begins. These gifts, through the power of the Holy Spirit, take on new weight and new meaning in that community. The money becomes God's work in that place, the bread becomes for us the body of Christ, and the wine becomes Christ's blood. We move from where we have been standing or kneeling, and we receive this fortified bread and wine. As we eat it, it becomes part of us.

We will carry this little bit of Jesus, the Christ out into the world with us. In a sense, we too become the body of Christ, for, at the end of the service, we are broken and distributed—that is, we go our own way into the world to feed others in Christ's name.

Out there in the world we give of ourselves for others, we learn, we share, and we grow. Sometimes we fall short of the mark and we sin. And on the next Sunday we return to that service again, we sing, we listen, we learn, we reaffirm our faith, we pray, we confess, we are forgiven, and we offer ourselves again as the gifts are collected and taken to the altar. God gives us back the money as the work of the church—something more than we offered. God gives us back the bread and wine and, in, with, and under them, the real presence of Christ—something more than we offered. God gives us back our lives, but gives them back fuller, healthier, more complete—something more than we offered. The circle is complete.

This is what the eucharist is about, and our job is to make the most of those things in our own services that are helpful and to make the least of those things which are not helpful to this poetic process.

Integrity of Focus

My ministry is in a large congregation in a room that seats hundreds, with sight lines as long as two hundred feet. It should be obvious that the lavabo used at that altar needs to be larger than one used in a chapel that seats twenty. The cruets need to be large enough to hold ample wine for the congregation. The gospel book should be of a size and dignity to command the attention of the congregation when it is brought into view. Vessels, vestments, and appointments should all have some relationship to the place where they are used, but in our time I think we need to look seriously at the focus of our worship. A friend of mine has a perfectly lovely Italian rococo crèche that sits beneath her Christmas tree. It is a joyful statement of the Incarnation done up in jewel-like colors and gold-leafed beyond reason. The barn has brackets of golden angels holding up the roof. The camels are wearing more jewelry than would be tasteful for Magi, and amidst all the fuss are a multitude of sheep, oxen, and wise men; also, some dancing, sitting, and giggling shepherds; the holy parents each with their own attendants; and the innkeeper, his wife, and some friends from down the street. In all this, we almost miss the small and unadorned child who lies quietly yet smiling in a wooden manger. There is so much stuff in the barn that it would be easy to miss God-with-us, Emmanuel.

I wonder if sometimes our worship is not like this crèche. I wonder if we have not gilded and embroidered and laced the edges of this sacramental meal to such an extent that sometimes we lose the bread and wine, simple gifts, the mix of all that surrounds them. I wonder if from time to time we need to look at the things we use in worship and how they speak to the focus of our worship. What things among them are doing exactly what we want them to do? What things are lacking in the weight and dignity that should be present? What things distract from the overarching experience of the eucharist? Does each piece of our table setting speak to its own function, or does it confuse the issue and focus of the meal? When our table is set for eucharistic worship is there a simple and unified statement of our unity? Is there one bread and one cup? Does the vessel for reserved wine look like something designed to hold wine? Does the chalice look like something from which we could actually drink? Does the paten or basket communicate that it is a place for bread? Is the table of an appropriate height and scale as to be approachable by human beings? Is it welcoming, well-lit, and inviting? Does it look as if friends might gather here to pray and offer the eucharist?

Integrity of Persons

One way to touch people at a different level of meaning without making a lot of changes in the local liturgy is to make some changes in the cast of characters. Of course we first must realize that we are a church with orders and that some jobs are assigned to people, not because of the virtues of their own personalities, but by virtue of their order of ministry. Bishops preside at the eucharist and preach the word. Priests serve vicariously for the bishop when he or she is absent. Deacons present the gospel to the congregation, set the table and call the people to prayer. Lay persons participate in the hymns, the responses, the psalms; they read the first two lessons and participate in the prayers; they serve chalices in the absence of sufficient priests and deacons; and they carry Christ out into the world.

What if we begin to look differently inside those established orders? What would be different if we assigned, for example, the job of reading the lessons to a couple of our most experienced and beloved Sunday school teachers? Would the words be heard in a different, if not clearer, way? If there is a really joyful storyteller in our congregation, who better to read to us, in worship, one of the stories of our faith? Who better to present the offerings and oblations of our lives and labors at the altar than one of the members of the stewardship committee or a member of the vestry or someone who is known as a generous giver in our congregation? At the time for the prayers of the people, who better to read the petitions of the people than someone among us who has a healthy and disciplined prayer life? Who better to bear the chalice at our altar than a member of our congregation who is actively involved in feeding the poor in the world?

You see, when we begin to choose members of our congregation for work in the church that reflects their lives in the world, then we begin to give credence and believability to what happens in church. All of a sudden, we are not stepping into God's world for an hour or two on Sundays, but recognizing that God has stepped into our own world, our own experience, not only in this hour, but in all our lives. This very subtle rearranging of the people who take responsibility for public worship in our churches can make a valuable difference in how we experience corporate worship. This integrity of persons can give a new integrity to our offerings of prayer and praise.

Integrity of Space

A friend of mine with an eye for historic architecture reminds me that, for at least the last couple of hundred years (and, of course, with some notable exceptions), we have not built buildings to fit our liturgies; rather, we have made our liturgies fit our buildings. We can tour the country and find hundreds of churches with architecture that suggests that the main service of the week is a choral presentation of the daily office, sung antiphonally by a split choir across a central aisle while the congregation interacts only as spectator to the event. The architecture remains intact, but I don't think we find that particular service actually happening in many places. What does happen in those buildings, especially since 1979 and its edition of the Book of Common Prayer, is at least a weekly service of eucharist in which the people assembled are called to participate more and more. What were originally decorations may now prove to be barriers to the way we worship. And although we Anglicans are much in love with our sacred precincts, there comes a time when we have to rethink how we are using a particular space. There is not room in this article for discussing how we can tailor our specific spaces to universal worship needs; suffice it to say that there needs to be some connection between the room used for worship and the kind of worship that happens in that room. [Ed. note: see "A Place of Good News: Liturgical Space as an Element in the Proclamation of the Gospel" by Charles Fulton and Juan Oliver, page 50.]

If we are a church that accepts all people equally, are we taking seriously the issue of physical accessibility to the different focal points of the room? Can a person confined to a wheelchair sing in the choir, read the Old Testament lesson, receive communion with his or her family? Can a person whose hearing is impaired take part in the prayers of the people, or the Nicene Creed? How do our buildings keep people from worshiping, and how can we rearrange them or redesign them so that all can equally approach the worship that is offered there?

Integrity of Form

Perhaps a gardening metaphor works best to explain the importance of the integrity of form in worship. I am an avid backyard gardener. I do not cling specifically to one form of gardening or another, but I know the differences when I see them. I am attracted to English country gardening with its stalky flowers, drippy vines, and bursts of colors, but I equally appreciate the more formal form of French gardening which seems to my eye more disciplined and exacting, dependent on symmetry, height and balance, using color in an almost secondary way. What makes me nervous or challenges my equilibrium is to see a garden that progresses in the French tradition, until the eye is surprised by a runaway bunch of hollyhocks that defy symmetry and discipline. Conversely, an English garden that is characteristically asymmetrical but devoid of the expected splashes of color looks like the back lot of the local nursery—like something preparing to happen rather than something dynamic and living.

So it is in our worship. We begin to feel off balance as we mix the forms of different periods and styles of language. Hymnody included in a particular service may run the gamut of four hundred years of composition, but all selections should be from a particular "mind set" of music. But two forms from the same Book of Common Prayer may not work at all in the context of a single service. My hope is that we take seriously the form of different parts of our service. If we are doing public baptism and our only baptismal rite is in contemporary language, then the eucharist which sets the context for that baptism would be best served by the contemporary language rite. When we are celebrating the eucharist using a more historic language, then we should take care when choosing the prayers of the people so as not jolt the people with a change of language.

Externally, we should be very careful about the inclusion of things which are not part of our worshiping heritage and equally careful about dropping or changing particular words of the eucharistic rites. Like it or not, we are bound together in a church that has agreed, through a grueling process, that these are the words of our worship when we are together, and to change these words outside this process seems to go against the spirit or our polity and our tradition.

As we enter now the era of Supplemental Liturgies, I think it will be even more important to protect the integrity of form in public worship. We have at our disposal so many wonderful options. Yet we must learn to use them well; otherwise our liturgies will look like they were gleaned from the leavings from some liturgist's lair!

Twenty Questions for Congregations in Liturgical Renewal

Having raised some issues with you about the way we worship and about some focuses that might be helpful, I invite you to review these questions in regard to your own community of worship. Do not be too critical. Whenever you can, start with something that works and think why it works and how it works. Then use the same sort of reasoning to get other things to work as well. Use these questions, not to fix your liturgical experience, but to nurture it to a more mature, more believable expression of our faith in a God who feeds us. That will give new integrity to our acts of worship, to our faith and, finally, to our lives.

- Does your congregation look at the eucharist as prose, that is, the sum of the details included in the service, or as poetry, which stresses the overarching themes of the service?

- Can the people responsible for designing liturgy in your congregation explain how the eucharist shapes their lives, and is that explanation congruent with the life of your congregation?
- When your worship is at its best, describe what happens from the end of the prayers of the people to the beginning of the eucharistic prayer.
- Would a stranger sitting in your congregation understand the symbolic weight of offertory as he or she sees it?
- How does your liturgy reflect the church's going out into the world to be the body of Christ there?
- Do the vessels, vestments, and appointments used in your liturgy bear a proper relationship to the room and congregation in which they are used?
- Do the vessels, vestments, and appointments used in your liturgy speak to their function by their appearance?
- Are lay people, deacons, priests, and bishops used in appropriate ways in the liturgical worship of your congregation?
- Are there some members of your congregation whose ministries there make them valuable assets as lectors? Oblation bearers? Leaders of the prayers? Lay eucharistic ministers?
- What are some other ways that we can show that Christian ministry is not necessarily learning a *new* skill but sharing an *old* gift?
- What changes in the way you have worshiped over the last fifteen years have resulted in changes in the way you use your building?
- What changes in the way you have worshiped over the last fifteen years have been caused by the shape of your building?
- What changes would be necessary to make your whole worship space equally accessible to people of varying physical abilities?
- In baptism liturgies or liturgies appointed for special days which are only available in contemporary language, does your congregation match the rest of its service to this language?
- If you are using Rite One of the Holy Eucharist, is care given to the choosing of prayers of the people that blend with that historic language?
- How might your congregation begin using some of the supplemental liturgies in your worship schedule?
- Describe the people you see at worship each Sunday. Do they seem truly happy to be there, and are they being fed by your church's liturgical worship?

- Are new people welcomed into the group mentioned in the question above, or does this group remain basically the same?
- How large is the group that is responsible for making liturgical decisions in your congregation? Is this congruent with the life of your church?
- Describe the absolute best service that you have seen in the last three years. What made it so good? Are there ways your congregation can incorporate some of these positive experiences into your weekly worship?

In Anglicanism, the liturgy is perhaps our best tool for evangelism. It is the way we express our theology. It is where we go for answers, for solace, for challenge, and for simply feeling God's presence. The law of prayer does yield the law of creed. Changing the way a congregation worships in subtle and pastoral ways may be a way to start new growth on any number of different levels. When people are being fed spiritually, when they begin cementing into community for no other reason than the faith which binds them, then you will know that your liturgy is working, that God is being served, and that the church is becoming God's people at prayer.

How to Plan Worship

by Juan Oliver

Liturgical planning is the process of making decisions concerning a wide variety of choices regarding the worship service of a particular congregation. The 1979 Book of Common Prayer gives unprecedented freedom to the persons planning the liturgy to make certain choices from time to time. As part of the process, the following questions will help the rector or vicar to make these decisions.

General Questions

- What are the overall values held by the congregation in relation to its ritual? Are there, in fact, different styles of worship in one congregation? Does this need to be expressed through a number of different liturgies, crafted differently?
- Do some of these values need to change through further pastoral care, formation, and education?
- How does the liturgical space facilitate good worship? How is the congregation aware of itself as the central symbol in the liturgy? Are the seating arrangements in keeping with a sense of the congregation as the main celebrant of the liturgy? How could the space itself contribute to or improve this perception?
- Is there a shift taking place in the congregation's understanding and "felt-sense" of the sacred?
- Is the range of music chosen appropriate to the congregation's sense of the sacred?
- Would a long-term member answer the questions above in the same way as a recently arrived member? Would the younger members answer in the same way as the older?

Seasonal Questions

- What changes in the use of sacred things will mark the passage of the church's seasons? How will the bread, wine, chalice(s), linens, flowers and decoration, vestments, incense, choice of musical accompaniment all conspire to form an indelible memory of the, let us say, "feel and taste of Easter"?

Weekly Questions

Since ritual is by nature conservative, most weekly decisions regarding the liturgy are rather minute, leaving large shifts for seasonal expression. Still, several questions need to be asked by liturgical planners week by week. Often these are handled *ad hoc* by the rector, music director, and altar guild without the immediate input from the worship committee.

- What music choices has the music director made? How will the rector evaluate them for approval? What is the relationship between the sung texts and the readings? Between sung texts and events in the life of the congregation and the rest of the world?
- Are there any events in the life of the congregation that must be specially highlighted this Sunday? For example, is this Stewardship Sunday? Was it chosen for this regardless of the readings or precisely because the readings are related to stewardship?
- Is the preacher aware of the musical choices made?
- Are there any specific changes in choreography or the use of ritual objects that need to be made on this particular Sunday?
- How can the prayers of the people best be crafted so as to relate the readings to the events of the past week and to the concerns of the congregation?

How to Introduce Full and Complete Use of Symbols

by Juan Oliver

Christian worship is an orchestrated and complex array of symbolic actions, involving bodies in a ritual space. Symbolic actions are expressive actions such as gathering, listening, praying, washing, eating, anointing, etc., which involve our bodies in relation to each other and to physical objects used in expressive ways. The worship service will be stronger when these modes of expression are engaged in fully without abbreviation. Thus, the full and complete use of symbolic actions and objects is important in order to preserve the expressive and formative character of the worship. Besides, the full and complete use of symbolic actions and objects often requires less interpretation and explanation than their abbreviated forms.

However, members of congregations often develop attachments to particular forms of abbreviation, such as pre-cut hosts, the diminutive baptismal bowl, or the silver ring filled with cotton and a dab of rancid oil. Often the display of these abbreviations is even equated with liturgical know-how!

Instead, a sensitive worship committee may gradually introduce into the worship of the congregation the full and complete use of symbolic actions, particularly as people generally find these much more moving and engaging than their abbreviated forms. Thus the worship committee might entertain questions such as:

- How may we better use an abundance of water in baptism to engage the washing and burial/rising images present in the rite?
- How may we better express the election/royalty/prophetic aspects of the baptismal anointing?
- In what ways would the shared meal aspects of the eucharist be brought to the fore by the use of a whole loaf of bread, easily recognizable as bread by all, and broken to feed all?
- How may the preacher(s) better engage the congregation in the act of reflecting upon the meaning of scripture for us today?

- How may the deacon or other leader best lead the people in their prayers for the church and the world? How may the leader best express and facilitate the priestly ministry of the assembly as it intercedes for the church and for the world?
- How may the congregation best act their priesthood through posture and placement during the eucharistic prayer without blurring the distinctions among orders of the church?
- How may the congregations best begin and enter into the liturgy of the word?
- How are moments of silence best employed? When?
- How can all the above be implemented gradually so that the congregation will celebrate these shifts rather than resent them?

Through these questions and many more of the same kind, a worship committee can make planning decisions which will enhance the expressive nature of worship and help our gathered congregations to manifest in tangible and audible forms God's reign already taking shape among us. It helps to keep in mind that a symbol is an expressive sign of something. When working in good order, symbols do not require explanation, for they make immediately available to the participants what they express. For this reason, pre-cut hosts, for example, do not work well as symbols; they obscure the sharing involved in eucharist by being pre-cut; they minimize the meal aspect of the rite by barely requiring chewing; and they usually require theological explanation, given that they fail to proclaim as simply and succinctly as would a loaf that "The Eucharist is a meal shared in memory of Christ in which He is revealed as present in us, His Body. For we though many, are One, for we share one bread."

How to Welcome Children in the Sunday Assembly

by Gretchen Wolff Pritchard

In a family, children are the treasured promise of the future, the focus of the family's love and hope. It is the children who are greeted first by visiting grandparents; it is the children whose faces fill the photograph albums, whose achievements and milestones, questions and concerns and needs are the focus of so much of the family's conversation, time, and resources. If the church is God's family, we should find in each parish community the same love and care, the same deep investment in nurturing and treasuring each child.

In a large congregation, even one that is very committed to its children, it can be hard for children to be visible, known, and treasured. A large congregation is often forced to incorporate the children into its common life in formal ways, in groups: Sunday school children present a pageant; a children's choir sings an anthem; a preschool class bakes the eucharistic bread; the youth group does a service project. In the small church, children can be incorporated more readily into the Sunday assembly in the casual, flexible way that is characteristic of family gatherings:

> John, two-and-a-half years old, and Catherine, four months old, came to worship with their parents. Catherine was asleep in her father's arms, and there were many offers to share his burden. There was a portable baby swing at the back of the sanctuary for Catherine in case she started to fuss. John brought paper, crayons, a stuffed dog, and a blanket. He settled himself and his belongings along the pew beside his parents. He did not remain there long. He was free to sit beside anyone in his wandering, but he attracted no special attention. During the sermon and prayers he was treated with a kind of benign neglect—helped, hugged, or ignored without much fuss or concentration. John joined in singing his version of the hymns and actually approximated the words of the Doxology. Once his hymn lasted longer than the congregation's. He copied the bowed heads in prayer for as long as five seconds. He stood by the end of the pew and placed his gift in the offering plate, then accompanied the usher to the front of the church. At the close of the service John stood by the minister and shook hands with people for a few minutes, then joined two older children who rolled a ball with him while his parents visited. Catherine, now awake, was admired and held. About half the congregation went home to John's house for iced tea.[28]

[28]"Beth-Salem Church, 38 members, in a rural community," from *Children in the Worshiping Community* by David Ng and Virginia Thomas (John Knox Press, 1981), p. 10.

The place of each child in the small parish can be unique and special; each child as an individual can be the treasured child of the whole parish family. How do we help this to happen?

In a family, the arrival of the first child or grandchild brings many changes, including changes in the way the family gathers for meals and holidays. A formal Thanksgiving dinner at 2:00 P.M. at a table set with china and crystal in a room full of fragile ornaments is not an appropriate form of celebration for a family with several young children. The family can choose to have the kids eat early and then nap or watch TV while the adults enjoy a leisurely meal. Or it can bring the children to the table and be prepared either to make some changes in how the meal is served or else to spend the entire time engaging in damage control. Sensitive families will choose to adapt, because adults and children alike know that it is the feast shared together that is the essence of the holiday. The children learn about the celebration by being part of it: anticipating, asking questions, sharing in preparations, welcoming guests or relatives, giving and receiving gifts, sitting at the family table, carrying on family traditions, hearing family stories, mugging for the camera, storing up memories.

The small church functions more like an extended family than an institution. Its smallness and intimacy encourage people of all ages to celebrate and learn together. Smallness and intimacy also place the Sunday liturgy in high prominence as the community's family celebration: Sunday worship is clearly what the family does together week by week; it is not just one among many busy activities and programs, as it may sometimes seem in a large parish. In a small community, separating the children from worship, especially eucharistic worship, sends a very clear message—like having the kids eat early on Thanksgiving Day. It tells the children that the family's defining moments routinely happen without them.

When children are participating, the family's forms of celebration need to take the children's presence into account. The same is true in the church. The first and guiding principle of incorporating children in liturgy is that the children's presence be acknowledged: the children must not be invisible, marginalized, or forgotten. Children in the liturgy are not guests or spectators at an adult event; they are members of the assembled family.

As the family assembles, children should be greeted and welcomed on the same basis as adults. If there are bulletins for each adult, there should be a bulletin (or a children's bulletin) for each child also—even the child who cannot read. When the offering plate is passed, it should never pass over the heads of young children as if they were not there. In a small parish where everybody knows everybody else's name, adults and children should know each other's names as well. Sam Gillespie deserves to be known as Sam, not "the younger of the Gillespie boys." And Sam needs to know that the lady behind the table at coffee hour is Mrs. Thomas or Marie—not "the cookie lady."

Children who are visible and included in the liturgy will be visible and included at the Lord's table. The eucharist is the birthright of every baptized child, however young. For the first thousand years and more of the church's history, children and babies routinely received communion as full members of the worshiping community; this practice has continued uninterrupted in the Orthodox churches and is now being rediscovered in the West. The sacramental meal is the daily bread of the family of God—there is no need to establish prerequisites for admission to it, or to set aside and celebrate a "first communion," or even to wait until children somehow express an active desire to receive, or demonstrate an awareness that the eucharist is "special" or different from an ordinary snack:

> We do not lecture children about the meaning of birthday parties before we give them a party, neither do we wait until they are able to understand all the facets of the ritual. We place the one-year-old child before a cake and presents, and in the midst of the celebration the child learns what birthday parties are.[29]

Babies in arms may receive communion in one kind only, sucking the wine from a finger dipped in the cup; or the parent may break off a small piece of the bread or wafer and then dip it in the cup and place it in the child's mouth. Most toddlers are entirely capable of receiving in both kinds, in the normal fashion. It may be awkward for the chalicist to administer the cup to very small children; this is easily handled by lifting the child briefly as the cup is given, so that the chalicist does not have to bend or squat down and can more easily tell when the child has received.[30]

Children who regularly receive communion show a natural and entirely appropriate reverence and eagerness for the sacrament, and rarely misbehave or cause any kind of disruption at the altar rail. Incorporating children in the eucharist itself is in fact the easiest part of incorporating children in parish liturgy. Children have a natural affinity for the symbolic language of sacrament: they understand intuitively the significance of setting a table, of offering and lifting up, of blessing, breaking, and giving. Our liturgy, however, is a liturgy of word as well as sacrament. We assemble in a space that is designed as much (or more) for sitting and listening as for celebrating; the lessons, sermon, prayers, and hymns were not framed with children's capacities in mind.

Probably the majority of Episcopal parishes do not expect children to be present for the liturgy of the word. Instead, they offer alternative programs: nursery care, children's chapel, Sunday school classes. Separating the assembly by age and role always risks being divisive, dispiriting, and damaging to the Sunday liturgy as a visible sign of the body of

---

[29] Gail Ramshaw, "The Pre-schooler in the Liturgy," from *The Sacred Play of Children,* Diane Apostolos-Cappadona, ed. (Seabury, 1983), p. 117.

[30] For further discussion of children and communion, see Gretchen Wolff Pritchard, *Offering the Gospel to Children* (Cowley, 1992), chapter 22.

Christ. These negatives may be minimized if the children's programs genuinely offer the same elements as the liturgy itself—praise, penitence, and prayer linked to the church's year, and an encounter with the word of God that is more than an academic exercise or a moral lesson—and if all the children, even babies from the nursery, join the full assembly no later than the offertory. For a small parish, however, a full children's program parallel to the liturgy of the word may be impossible or impractical. The building may have no appropriate space; there may be insufficient or unpredictable numbers of children in each age group; or (most likely of all) there may not be enough adults who are able or willing to be absent from the liturgy to lead children's programs.

There are ways to meet the challenge of the liturgy of the word, so that children and adults together can experience the entire Sunday service as a family:

> Could what we often consider problems be assets? What could a child's awareness of the sanctuary and its symbols add to our worship? Could their motion and rhythm expand our understanding of worship beyond "sitting still"? What if their humor flavored our sobriety, their vocabulary limitations sharpened our communication, and their need for the concrete made visible our abstractions? . . . A vital element in all ages worshiping together is this wedding of adult and childhood gifts in our corporate liturgy. Our differences become a rich harmony.[31]

Our liturgy uses space, words and music. Attention to each of these elements in the light of children's special needs and gifts will help the family to incorporate children fully, to the benefit of all.

The specific issues raised by the size, shape, and quality of the worship space vary enormously from parish to parish. A rural congregation with a tiny building faces different challenges from a downtown parish that is small in numbers but assembles each Sunday in a colossal Victorian nave, a relic of long-vanished urban gentility. Too little space makes children squirm; too much makes them zoom, while a dark and looming space with few people in it may feel very unsafe to small children. Their basic needs are for clear sight lines, clear physical boundaries, and, within those boundaries, opportunity both for intimacy (hugs, cuddles, and whispered conversations) and for a certain amount of free movement, including the chance to draw or write and the chance to lie down. Ideally, there should be two concentric sets of boundaries, one defined by the child's own family group and another somewhat larger area in which children are free to migrate between different family groups without escaping entirely, evading adult control, feeling lost or overwhelmed, endangering themselves or disrupting others.

Despite the bad press that traditional pews have received from the liturgical movement, they handily meet all the criteria for the first level of physical enclosure and are generally much more child-friendly than chairs (especially lightweight folding chairs or contoured plastic chairs), as long as the family sits fairly close to the front. Children can

---

[31]Ng and Thomas, *Children in the Worshiping Community*. p. 16.

stand on the kneeler or the pew itself for a better view, kneel on the floor to use the pew as a desk, spread out their belongings, change places within the family group, move closer or further away from parents and siblings, or stretch out on the pew for some "down time" with bottle or thumb and blanket, all with a minimum of fuss and disturbance. Providing an effective secondary level of enclosure is more difficult. One possibility is a rug on the floor between the front pew and the communion rail, on which children can sit or lie down if sight lines from the pews are poor. In a cavernous space in which children run wild or feel overwhelmed, whole sections may simply be roped off, to create a more human scale. In general, however, the larger worship space cannot be fully "child-proofed" by physical features alone. The congregation itself needs to provide the second ring of enclosure, the safe and loving space in which children are free to move but always safely held.[32]

If we are sensitive to children's need for certain kinds of freedom of movement in church, we will find clues to their characteristic ways of encountering the forms of our worship: its words and music. For adults, participating in the service means "paying attention"—sitting up, eyes on the celebrant or preacher or reader, all mental powers focused and engaged, all bodily motion stilled. It means "following the service"—saying the correct responses, standing and kneeling at the right times, singing the hymns. Any other forms of behavior are perceived as "inattention," and we decide that the child has failed, or the liturgy has failed, because the child is not paying attention. So we resort to separate children's liturgies, and to children's sermons, skits, puppets, and other devices to elicit the kind of spellbound attention that we have seen children give to good teachers and to television and other forms of entertainment.

But liturgy, like much repetitive ritual, does not necessarily function in the same way as do entertainment and instruction:

> The liturgy teaches by immersing us into a juxtaposition of images, stories, and symbols of the faith. . . . This mingling of imagery makes the liturgy accessible to small children whose fantasy life has not yet been tied down by the bonds of analytic logic. Tuning in and out of the liturgy, small children can immediately grab a floating image and fly with it or remember it the next day in private reverie and creative play.[33]

Many of the behaviors children exhibit in church—wandering, imitating, cuddling, daydreaming, lying down with thumb and blanket, doodling—are precisely the mechanisms by which they process ritual material. Powerful words and images are washing over them; when we insist that they engage these images in ways adults consider appropriate, we may actually impede them from making their own response. A child who is lying on

[32]For more on preparing worship space to encourage children's participation in the liturgy, see Pritchard, *Offering the Gospel to Children*, chapter 21.

[33]Ramshaw, "The Pre-schooler in the Liturgy," p. 117.

the pew staring into space or doodling in the bulletin may be engaged in authentic prayer or meditation, far more deeply involved with the liturgy than a child who is exhibiting the "correct" posture and speaking the responses at the correct times. Prayer and meditation are quite different from reading, speaking, and following a text. The effort needed to do one may entirely crowd out the other, whereas a right-brain activity like drawing may free the mind to listen and to ponder.[34] There are plenty of adults, after all, who cannot truly pray as long as their eyes are focused on the words on the page, but must memorize prayers and responses so that they are able to shut their eyes; only then can they pray the words rather than merely say them.

Much of what appears to be inattention, however, is exactly that: inattention. Children are self-centered, easily bored, and easily distracted. Especially in the intimacy of a small community, children need to be taught self-control and consideration for others, and they need to be encouraged to see that the liturgy is for them as well as to feel it washing over them. This will only happen if the entire community is sensitized to children's needs. Parents as well as other adults need to see the children as fellow worshipers rather than as guests or intruders. It takes positive effort to learn to respond to deteriorating behavior not with discipline ("Stop that! Be quiet!") or even with distraction (a toy, a cookie), but with evangelism and nurture— gently working to re-engage the child with the liturgy. Sometimes it will be necessary to take a disruptive child out of the assembly for a cooling-off period. Clear ground rules are needed as to when and how this should be done—and how the child should re-enter when the crisis is past.[35]

It will help the children if the celebrant establishes eye contact with them as well as with adults; if the preacher uses stories and concrete imagery as well as erudite vocabulary and abstract concepts; if children are invited, according to their ability, to assist as ushers and readers as well as acolytes; and if they are occasionally invited forward to see closely what the celebrant is doing. (This custom should not be restricted to baptisms, as if baptism were still the "children's sacrament" in a way that the eucharist is not.) Variable and optional elements in the liturgy should be used with care and sensitivity for those who cannot read; for example, Form IV of the Prayers of the People, with its repeated refrain, invites children's participation far more than Form III or Form VI, in which each petition requires a different response. Frequent shifting between different options such

[34]For more on children's doodles in church, see Pritchard, *Offering the Gospel to Children,* chapter 10.

[35]An extremely full discussion of strategies for helping the congregation welcome children to the whole liturgy is found in *Going to Church with Children,* by Stan Stewart, Pauline Stewart, and Richard Green, Melbourne, Australia, Joint Board of Christian Education (JBCE), 1987. At this writing, this excellent book is not available in the United States. Morehouse Publishing has recently begun issuing titles from the JBCE; interested readers may wish to check with Morehouse concerning the possibility of an American edition.

as Rite One and Rite Two, the contemporary and traditional Lord's Prayer, or even the different eucharistic prayers with their different memorial acclamations, multiplies difficulties for young children—though school-age children may enjoy the challenge of learning the ropes.

Many of the same considerations apply to music. It is helpful to young children if some of the music is the same every week, allowing them to learn it by heart. In hymns, children appreciate strong rhythms, major keys, and clear structure, especially refrains. Simplicity of lyrics is a lesser concern. A grand tune can seduce children into a fruitful engagement with a rich and complex text, whereas many "children's hymns" are characterized more by bland or condescending lyrics than by genuinely singable music. (How many children—or adults—can correctly sing the tune of "The Butterfly Song" or "Day by Day"?) Hymns that have been old favorites for generations will continue to be loved and treasured; folk tunes, spirituals, and traditional carols are a good place to start in introducing new music.

Incorporating children into parish worship requires work—work by those who plan worship and those who lead it; not only the priest but also the reader, the chalicist, the usher; those who are not parents as well as those who are. Planning and sensitivity, and the firm conviction that children are a heritage and gift from the Lord and belong in the worshiping assembly, will go a long way to smooth the rough spots from the parish Sunday liturgy. Rough spots, however, will remain. No family celebration, no family life, is made up entirely or even mostly of golden moments. The picture-perfect Thanksgiving dinner dissolves into spilled milk and cold gravy; the noise level rises; the sink fills with dirty dishes. Children squabble, babies fuss and scream, and the two-year-old climbs the furniture and rubs cranberry sauce into his hair. The family of God meeting Sunday by Sunday is equally subject to the weaknesses of the flesh. But it is through flesh that God chooses to come to us. Paul may recommend that all be done decently and in order, but it is Jesus who welcomed the children.

How to Design Service Leaflets Which Are Helpful to the Newcomer

by Marilyn L. Haskel

Service leaflets can be used for the simple purpose of giving page numbers of hymns and parts of the liturgy, thus eliminating disruptive announcements; or they may be easily transformed into a tool of hospitality and education for the newcomer, the casual visitor to worship, the unchurched, or the physically challenged. Second only to the warmth of greeting by members of the parish, the accessibility of the worship leaflet is perhaps the single most important vehicle for welcoming people. For someone unfamiliar with Anglican liturgical form and practices, our worship is often complex and confusing. Clear instructions about standing, sitting, and kneeling are, perhaps, the most basic aids. This can be accomplished with the rubrics *Please stand* or *You may stand or kneel* or *Remain seated* printed clearly at the appropriate places in the liturgy.

Stating the color of the various books to be used is also helpful. Hymnal page numbers could be listed at the left margin with Prayer Book pages listed at the right, such as:

THE WORD OF GOD

Prelude	Prelude and Fugue in C	J. S. Bach
Red Hymnal		*Blue Prayer Book*
Please stand		
390	Praise to the Lord, the Almighty	
Greeting		355
Collect for Purity		
S274	Glory to God	
The Collect of the Day		357
Please be seated		
The Lessons		

Using title design and type size similar to those in the Book of Common Prayer is essential for clarity. For example, for "The Holy Eucharist: Rite Two," the Prayer Book uses the largest titles for the two divisions of worship: "The Word of God" and "The Holy Communion." Other parts of the liturgy are indicated in bold but smaller type.

Many churches also list some parts of the service by title even though the Prayer Book does not, i.e., The Lord's Prayer. With regard to Latin words such as "Gloria in excelsis" or "Sanctus," it is important to remember that it would be helpful for the newcomer to see the English translation. As a way to educate, it would be best to use both languages, as *The Hymnal* does: Glory to God, (*Gloria in excelsis*). This is also an excellent way to teach children about our heritage.

When printing the simple outline of the service with page numbers and limited rubrics for standing and sitting, it is helpful for the rubrics to be in a different typeface (italics or a slightly smaller type size). The use of many fonts is not recommended. To highlight, use bold printing, boxes, or underlining. The key is moderation.

If your most frequent newcomer is essentially unchurched, you may want to include a bit more information in the leaflet which would serve as an explanation about the various parts of the service. To keep the leaflet from looking cluttered and making it difficult to follow, it is recommended that this kind of information be very concise and printed in such a way that the notations do not distract attention from the body of the service order. This can be accomplished as follows:

Please exchange this ancient greeting with each other.	The Peace *All stand*	BCP 360
	THE HOLY COMMUNION	
The gifts of bread, wine, and money are brought to the altar.	The Offertory	
	Hymn: On Jordan's bank *Remain standing*	Hymnal 76
	The Great Thanksgiving	BCP 361
	Holy, holy, holy *Sanctus*	Hymnal S124

In the far left column are explanations of what will happen. Rubrics for standing and sitting could be included here also rather than in the body of the leaflet order.

If you use an abbreviation or initials for something, be sure that these are explained before they are used. For example, if you use BCP for Book of Common Prayer, indicate that in an explanatory paragraph at the beginning of the leaflet. Also, explain that the "S" numbers designate service music, found in the front section of *The Hymnal.*

The most helpful leaflet, of course, is one that prints the entire service. While this would seem to be a lot of work, the accessibility of computers has made this a more reasonable possibility than in the past. It allows participation by the physically challenged who may have difficulty managing books. It facilitates an enormous flexibility within the liturgy and gives the most support to those unfamiliar with the service.

If you were to use the format cited above, a description of the various parts of the eucharistic prayer could be incorporated in the left column notes, i.e., (Anamnesis) We remember Christ's sacrifice for us; (Words of institution) These are the words that originally established this celebration; (Oblation) We offer the gifts of bread and wine; (Invocation) We ask the Holy Spirit to make these gifts sacred; (Doxology) We praise the Father, Son, and Holy Spirit.

Another helpful teaching device is to include a brief note each week at the beginning of the leaflet which draws attention to specific events within the liturgy either weekly or seasonally. This might look like:

ABOUT OUR WORSHIP

In today's liturgy we will commission the Hospital Ministry Team. These parishioners have been trained to make daily pastoral visits to area hospitals and report to our clergy, who will do a follow-up visit.

The hangings and vestments today are blue for this season of Advent. They will remain until the Christmas liturgies.

Many parishes are concerned about the consumption of large quantities of paper if the entire liturgy is printed. It is possible to print all the text, some musical selections (such as the Gloria, Fraction Anthem, etc.) with page numbers for hymns on one sheet of 11" x 17" paper that is tri-folded lengthwise. This is, perhaps, the most economical. However, it will not provide room for weekly announcements or scripture texts. Those would need to be inserted on a half sheet of 8½" x 11" which would fit inside the tri-folded service leaflet. The lengthwise format also allows for enlarging a few copies for the visually impaired. (*The Hymnal 1982* is also available in a large print format from Church Hymnal Corporation.)

The Book of Common Prayer, *The Book of Occasional Services*, *Lesser Feasts and Fasts*, and *Supplemental Liturgical Materials* (1996) are available in a new CD-ROM version from the Church Hymnal Corporation so that creating a varied liturgy using many options is possible without a lot of data entry.

The goal is to be helpful and clear for the newcomer. Many of those who are not "cradle Episcopalians" remember the first time they worshiped in an Episcopal church. Often they believe that if they could persevere in understanding the liturgy, then anyone should do the same. However, a well-designed leaflet is not a detriment to those who may not require it, but it is invaluable to those who do.

How to Compose and Perform Intercessions

by Ormonde Plater

For the prayers of the people in the eucharist, or general intercessions, the Prayer Book provides several models. These include a form for Rite One (BCP, pages 328–330) and six forms for general use (BCP, pages 383–393). A parish may also compose its own forms for each Sunday and feast, for the seasons of the church year, and for special occasions.

Composing Intercessions

Composing the prayer is the job of a committee or one person with special skills in liturgical composition. The committee should include the deacons of the parish, if any, and others who minister to the poor, sick, and needy. Someone skilled in writing may draft the prayer.

There are six principles to follow in designing intercessions:

- They are *inclusive*. They cover the church, the world, the nation, the community, the suffering, and the dead.
- They are *general*. They ask God to have mercy on all those in need, not just a few special persons and concerns. Except on occasions such as weddings and funerals, it is better to announce special intentions before the intercessions.
- They are *intercessions*. We pray for the relief of needs, the remedy of concerns, the fulfillment of hopes. It is better to leave praise and thanksgiving to other parts of worship.
- They are *popular*. At the urging of a leader, the people pray. Several forms in the Prayer Book address God in terms such as "Father, we pray." The ancient tradition is for the leader to act as a herald, reminding the people of topics and asking them to pray.
- They are *simple*. Short biddings help the people to grasp the topic. They are also few in number—nine to twelve on Sundays and major feasts, four to six on weekdays.

- They are *responsorial.* After each bidding, the people respond with brief petitions. Long or variable responses force them to read from a book or paper. They need to look up, see the leader and each other, the altar, an icon or statue, and feel free to hold hands or raise them in prayer.

The form of intercessions is threefold: a brief invitation by the presider; biddings and responses; a concluding prayer by the presider. Among several ancient formulas for biddings are:

- "For [persons or concerns]."
- "That [intention]."
- "For [persons or concerns], that [intention]."

Biddings may end abruptly or, to cue the response, with a phrase such as "let us pray to the Lord." For the last bidding, the leader may ask us to join our voices with Mary and all the saints and commend ourselves to God (see Forms I and V).

The drafter or committee may also compose the invitation and collect. These may reflect the day (Sunday or feast), season, or occasion.

Performing Intercessions

Deacons and others who lead intercession are part of the leadership of a congregation. The people need to see them and hear them.

There are two main places to lead intercession: the lectern or ambo; and in the midst of the congregation. The place should suit the worship space and the customs of the worshipers. The people may form a circle around the altar, focus on an icon or other point of prayer, or stand at their seats. The presider may stand at one side of the assembly or at the chair, with the leader of intercession at the other side.

Following the presider's invitation, the leader or others in the congregation may read a few special intentions. These may include the Anglican and diocesan cycles of prayer, baptism and wedding anniversaries, the sick, and the dead. The leader may then invite the people to offer their own names and concerns, silently or aloud.

When the biddings take the form of a litany, it is especially desirable to sing them. The leader sings either the whole bidding or the ending phrase (or someone else sings the ending). The people sing their response in unison or harmony. After a response such as "Lord, have mercy," they may continue to hum during the next bidding.

By tradition, deacons (when functioning liturgically) lead the intercessions, but they often involve other baptized persons in the performance. Several different persons may announce special intentions beforehand, lead the biddings, or say (or sing) different parts of the biddings. If they minister to those in need in the church and the world, as well as in liturgy, their ministry in intercession will reveal the power and authority of God.

How to Celebrate the Triduum

by Michael Merriman

To celebrate the Triduum well we need first to remember that the rites of Maundy Thursday through Easter should be seen as one complex liturgy rather than as a collection of separate liturgies. While each rite has its own individual characteristics, each needs to be seen in this larger context.

The Triduum begins with the evening eucharist on Maundy Thursday which is the liturgy for the eve of Good Friday. In other words, we follow the biblical way of measuring days in which each day begins at sunset. Therefore Friday has two major liturgies (leaving out, for the moment, the daily office): the Maundy Thursday eucharist and the liturgy of Good Friday. It would be a mistake to overload the twenty-four-hour period from sunset on Thursday to sunset on Friday with any additional eucharists. Similarly, if too much ceremonial and musical energy is expended on Thursday, the Friday liturgy will suffer by comparison even though it should be clearly the primary service in that twenty-four-hour period.

It would seem to be best to make the Thursday evening eucharist a modest one in terms of music and ceremony. Medieval notions that it celebrates the institution of the eucharist or of the priesthood need to be shed. The footwashing in response to the preferred gospel reading as the final preparation of the faithful to participate in the paschal celebration should be central. As the eucharist of the eve of Good Friday, it should be restrained. Passiontide red or lenten vestments should be worn. The entrance rite should not include the *Gloria in excelsis* (many places find either the "Penitential Order" or the "Order of Worship for the Evening" to be the best way to begin). Music might be unaccompanied. Flowers should not be used. There should not be a blessing or dismissal; the people can depart in silence from the church or from the place where the remaining sacrament had been taken. This emphasizes that the liturgy is not over; we are simply leaving to return for more of it on Good Friday.

For Roman Catholics, the three-hour service of the past was intended to provide a popular devotional addition to an incomprehensible Latin service. For Anglicans, it provided a fuller service than the sketchy service outline that appeared in older editions of the Prayer Book. Therefore the present Good Friday liturgy removes the need for the three-hour service. This service should take place at a time convenient to most parishioners. It does not have to be from noon to 3:00 P.M. and, in most places, should not be. While the Good Friday liturgy should be restrained, the use of movement and music ought to underscore it as the primary service in that twenty-four hour period. The presentation of a wooden cross or crucifix (BCP, page 281) and the bringing of the reserved sacrament into the assembly should be accompanied by candles, music, and (if desired) incense. The people depart in silence without a blessing or dismissal.

Preparations and rehearsals for the Vigil service often require that the altar guild, liturgical ministers, catechumens, musicians, and many others gather in the worship space on Saturday. This gathering constitutes a ready-made congregation for the Holy Saturday rite (BCP, page 283). The service could include music for the psalm, a hymn before the gospel, and the singing of the anthem "In the midst of life" (see *The Hymnal 1982 Service Music* accompaniment book, S379, S382). For a homily, see the "ancient homily on the holy and great Sabbath" (*The Prayer Book Office*, page 735; see "For Further Reading" on page 156). Again all depart in silence without blessing or dismissal. Note that—as is appropriate for the day in which our Lord lay in the tomb—there is little that the church does liturgically other than prepare for the Vigil.

The Vigil should be the parish's primary Easter service. This is the service in which the greatest resources of music and ceremony are used: full choir, other musical instruments, all the flowers and best vestments, and a lavish coffee hour or party following (other services on that day, if needed, make do with what is still available). While in some places it will be necessary to celebrate this service on Saturday evening, that should happen after dark. It is far better to celebrate this service early on Sunday morning, beginning before sunrise, while it is still dark if possible. Parents can be encouraged to bring children along with blankets and pillows so that they can nap during the Vigil. When the baptisms and eucharist begin, they will wake up. Certainly, for the sake of the child in all of us, use "holy noise"—bells, organ, trumpets—when the Gloria or other hymn of praise begins. Many places find the hymn "This is the feast of victory" (Hymn 417, *The Hymnal 1982*) a good alternative to the Gloria, especially if there is a procession of the congregation into the area for the eucharist, because the choir can sing the verses with everyone joining on the refrain.

How to Introduce Baptism by Immersion

by Clayton L. Morris

The single most important rationale for the introduction of immersion in the baptismal rite is that principle of the importance of expansiveness of the use of symbols. A pool of water is a more potent symbol than a small bowlful. Pushing a human being beneath the surface of a pool of water is, obviously, a more potent symbolic act that sprinkling a bit of dampness onto the candidate's forehead. The "For Further Reading" section on page 152 refers to several resources which discuss the symbolism of water in baptism. This essay explores a strategy for introducing the expansive use of water in baptism.

The adult catechumenate is a process being used in an increasing number of congregations to structure the process of initiating adults into the body of Christ. When the initiation of an adult engages the ongoing life of a congregation, the baptismal process takes on a particular urgency. As the adult seeker inquires about the nature of life in the congregation and seeks to discern whether or not baptism is an appropriate response to the process of inquiry, the congregation is naturally drawn into an examination of the meaning and import of baptism. The baptismal event concluding the process becomes an important moment of renewal for the entire community.

The focused quality of this process suggests that the baptism of an adult catechumen is the most powerful possibility for the introduction of immersion as the baptismal technique. The adult seeker, coming into the community in hope of finding a locus for ministry, will be eager to make the most of the baptismal moment. The "dying-and-coming-to-life-again" experience of baptismal renewal demands the fullest possible use of the baptismal symbol.

Even in the more frequent circumstance of the baptism of an infant or small child, the use of a large quantity of water is meaningful. In fact, it may be easier to reintroduce ample water into such baptisms. Everyone loves children, especially babies. As the occasion of baptism arises in the congregation, consider asking parents about the possibility of immersion.

The preparations for an immersion baptism of a small child are simple. All that is required is a basin large enough to get the child into the water. It can be easily placed on a table. The temperature of the water can be controlled. The baby will love the care given by parents and sponsors who lovingly undress the child, wrap it in a soft towel or blanket for presentation to the baptizer. The warm water will soothe the infant, and a massage with holy oil will complete the experience.

The use of ample amounts of water in baptism can take several forms. One can lower someone into a pool of water. This is the appropriate method for infants (and the most dramatic method for any candidate). It is also possible to pour copious amounts of water over a candidate standing in a place where the water can be collected or will drain away easily. In the case of infants and small children (young enough to be held), a bath-like experience is the easiest to manage. In the case of an adult, if it is impossible to manage a pool in which the candidate can be immersed, then the pouring of enough water over the candidate to create the dramatic symbolic impression is a good alternative.

Involving a number of people in the process will help the community to come to terms with this new way of managing the initiatory sacrament. Ask several people to participate in the construction of the font. Ask others to discuss the best way of leading candidates and sponsors through the specific choreography of baptismal experience. They will want to consider questions such as:

- What should the candidate wear before the baptism and after?
- What is the best temperature for the water?
- How does the candidate get into and out of the font?
- What is the role of sponsors?
- Is it OK to baptize babies without clothes?

These are, in their essence, questions of hospitality. What can be done by representatives of the community to make the baptismal candidate, family, and sponsors familiar and comfortable with the experience?

The church is slowly recovering the essential, transformational nature of the sacrament of baptism. This reformation of baptismal theology deserves to be accompanied by a lavish use of the primary baptismal symbol. The copious use of water in the celebration of baptism enables the supporting community to recover a vital, baptismal context for the church's overall ministry.

The congregation wishing to explore baptism by immersion will have questions, probably many questions. The best place to look for answers to the specific, practical questions of strategy and procedure is a congregation already engaged in the full use of water. If such a congregation cannot be located nearby, call the Office for Liturgy and Music at the Episcopal Church Center for some suggestions.

How to Build a Baptismal Font

by Clayton L. Morris

The first Christian baptisms most certainly took place in streams of running water. Every Anglican Prayer Book since 1549 has assumed immersion as the preferred method. And, while immersion has been rare in the recent history of the Episcopal Church, it is attracting interest, especially in communities which are seriously engaged in exploring the implications of the baptismal covenant.

As the church recovers the notion that ministry in and to the world is the primary task of the baptized community, interest in the baptismal event increases. Since baptism is about washing and resurrection, the use of copious amounts of water in the baptismal liturgy is the natural result of this renewed understanding of the church's mission. But most Episcopal churches currently in use were built with the assumption that baptism required only a cup or so of water held in a small bowl or diminutive font. And so, the congregation seeking to exploit the symbolism of water in its baptismal rite is faced with the need to provide a new kind of baptismal font.

A number of congregations around the church have built fonts out of plywood with a watertight, fiberglass lining. Others have purchased livestock watering troughs from farm-supply stores. Still others have purchased ready-made baptismal font kits from evangelical church supply companies. Each of these options has helpful and unhelpful features.

The wooden font, constructed on site, is relatively inexpensive and is not difficult to build. Care must be taken to build the box with sufficient strength to contain a large quantity of water. The plywood box requires reinforcement to prevent the seams from splitting. The most difficult part of the project is the task of sealing the font with fiberglass, which is unpleasant to handle. The major difficulty in using these simple fonts is that they need to be drained by syphon.

The livestock trough is a durable, easily moved font which can be painted or decorated with ease. It can be fitted with a drain. It may, however, be difficult to find a trough which is tall enough to allow an adult to kneel into the water easily.

The ready-made baptismal font kit is an almost effortless solution to the problem. These kits can be purchased with drains, heaters, stairs, a variety of exterior "shells," covers, etc., which makes them easy to acquire and use.

Clearly, retrofitting a worship space with an immersion font is a task that is either labor-intensive or costly or, perhaps, both. The project involves serious consideration of a variety of issues. But as the most effective means to celebrate the sacrament of baptism in the most affectively persuasive way, and it is worth the effort!

An added benefit to congregational life for the community exploring baptism by immersion is the sense of ownership of the process achieved when members of the congregation build the font. While commercial alternatives to a "home-made" font are available, there is much to be said in favor of a gathering of folks crafting the font locally.

Before installing a temporary font, care should be taken to determine that the weight of the water will not create an excessive load on the structure of the building. Usually, a platform set across the joists of a wooden floor is adequate to distribute the weight, but professional advice should be sought in case of doubt.

If circumstances make it impossible to consider an immersion font, congregations might want to consider providing a baptismal place at which water can be poured over the candidates. Hardware stores or sheet metal fabricators can supply a simple pan, which can be placed on the floor, perhaps lined with carpeting. The baptismal candidate stands in the pan while water is poured over head and body. The water collects in the pan. Even a child's wading pool could be pressed into service in this circumstance. In this situation, it would not be unreasonable to offer baptism by pouring for adults, and immersion for infants and small children, assuming that even if a full-sized immersion font is impossible, a table-top font made of a metal wash tub can be provided.

A number of practical concerns will come to light as preparations for baptism by immersion proceed. Decorating the exterior of the font can be accomplished in a number of ways. If the need is to hide the rough surface of a wooden font or steel trough, a lining of chicken wire can be affixed to the perimeter of the font to serve as a holder for greens and flowers. Or, a fabric "curtain" can be created to provide a decorative covering. The exterior surface of the font can be painted, perhaps with representations of the scripture readings from the Easter Vigil or baptismal lections. Iconic images, perhaps painted by church school classes, could be attached to the exterior of the font.

Unless the font has its own heater, a supply of hot water will need to be provided. One solution is to fill the font from a water heater, using a garden hose attached to a sink in a nearby utility room. It is likely that the water heater's supply will be exhausted before the font is full, so a practice run will be important that first time the font is used. If the font needs to be filled at a significant interval before the liturgy, a foam pad floated on the surface of the water will reduce the loss of heat.

Before a font is filled, care must be taken that the interior surface be absolutely clean. Any small bits of debris or oily residue clinging to the floor and walls of the interior will float to the surface of the water as it is filled. Consideration might be given to installing a circulating pump in the font. Not only does the sound and motion of moving water recall the early church's insistence on baptisms in *living water,* but the pump's filter will help keep the water clean.

Clearly, draining the font is easiest if a garden hose can be attached to a drain at the bottom of the tank. If a drain is not installed, water can be syphoned to a drain or garden plot with a hose. Some bailing likely will be necessary before the font can be moved easily.

The location of the font probably will be the result of compromise between ideal placement and architectural considerations. In warm climates, an outdoor installation might solve the problem of placement where the building does not allow space. In cold climates, where space limitations don't allow for the use of a large font in the church, perhaps the baptismal portion of the liturgy should occur in the parish hall or another more open space.

The Roman Church has taken the lead among sacramental denominations in the installation of permanent baptismal fonts. The congregation exploring the idea of baptism by immersion would do well to visit some good examples. While the trend toward the installation of fonts as an element in the design of new (and renewed) buildings is a hopeful sign, it is probably good for a congregation exploring the idea to begin with a temporary solution, so that questions of design and use will be thoroughly explored before architects and designers are engaged.

These days, the church is struggling with the notion that worship is formative ("praying shapes believing"). The church is also becoming increasingly aware that worship is most effective when it engages all five senses. When water is allowed to become a powerful and even dangerous symbol in the baptismal rite, the centrality of Christian Initiation to the life of the church is dramatically expressed. Thus, providing an immersion font is not just a decision to altar congregation habit, but participated in the process of transforming a worshiping community's experience of the church's mission.

How to Use Incense

by Clayton L. Morris

The use of incense in worship is ancient, certainly predating Christianity. There is no liturgical practice more firmly rooted in scripture than the use of incense; the image of fire and smoke is a common one in the Bible, constantly reminding the reader of scripture of the exodus of Israel from Egypt.

Incense has been used consistently since the sixth century, but not without controversy. The early church avoided the use of incense because of its connection with pagan religion and its use in civil ceremony. The post-Reformation church has sometimes shunned incense out of a need to avoid "papist" practices. One may wonder why Anglicans have allowed this captivity of such a powerful element of liturgical symbolism.

The sense of smell is perhaps the most powerful sense for the suggestion of memory. Adding a distinctive aroma to the liturgical event makes a strong suggestion to the worshiper that something of importance is taking place. Where there is smoke, there is fire, literally and figuratively! The presence of incense, in addition to its mythical and historical associations, enables one to remain alert and attentive.

Traditionally, there are two uses of incense associated with liturgy: censing as a gesture of devotion, and censing as a gesture of honor. The latter use is, perhaps, more central to the eucharistic celebration. In each case it signifies the holiness of certain ordinary objects, actions, and especially people. Incense may be carried at the head of the procession. The table and the bread and wine can be censed at the offertory. The congregation may be censed. Or, incense can be used as a symbolic representation of the "rising" prayers of the faithful (see Psalm 141:2 and Revelation 8:3–4).

The church has developed, over time, an elaborate ceremonial to accompany the use of incense, but it is not necessary to adhere to that pattern, nor is a complicated use of incense recommended. Incense carried in procession or used as an honorific gesture to people, to the gospel, or to the eucharistic elements should be done simply and directly.

As an alternative to carrying incense in a thurible, there are many occasions for which incense sprinkled on charcoal burning in a stationary brazier provides just the right accent. The smoke rises gently as the incense burns.

The issues of incense and allergy *can* be addressed. Here are some suggestions:

- When buying incense, make sure to procure pure resins. The addition of floral essence (dried flower petals, for example) and the presence of talc or sawdust (sometimes added to prevent grains of incense from sticking together) produce irritating smoke. Pure grains of pitch, crushed if necessary because of their size, will burn cleanly and, usually, without allergic reaction.
- Be careful to choose charcoal of quality, which burns without odor. Be certain that it is kept dry. Damp charcoal doesn't burn cleanly. Don't buy more than can be used in a reasonable length of time.
- Be certain that the thurible is kept clean. The burning and reburning of residue is irritating. Lining the bowl with foil is one way to facilitate the cleaning process.
- If it is necessary to limit the amount of smoke produced, consider using a thurible with bells on the chains. The ringing of the bells adds to the drama of the censing and compensates for the absence of voluminous amounts of smoke.
- Gathering wood resin can be an exercise for the local community. If there are trees in the neighborhood which yield pitch naturally, gather and dry it for use in the parish thurible.
- For communities eager to introduce the use of incense where it hasn't been part of the liturgical experience, Epiphany is a good time:
  - Use the gift of the Magi as a rationale for introducing some thoughts about the history of incense, its use in the ancient world, and its use in liturgy.
  - Use the Sundays after the Epiphany to experiment.
- Take the congregation on an olfactory tour of their own remembrances of fragrances —baking bread, cookies, or pumpkin pie; growing jasmine or dahlias; purchasing Easter lilies or Christmas trees, etc.; note what effect these have on their memories of certain events.

Singing a *New* Song: Not Always Easy!

by Mark T. Engelhardt

But we don't want to learn any new hymns. We like singing the old ones!

I wish I had a nickel for every time I've heard these words when the subject of learning new hymns arises. Before we can address the *how* of teaching new hymns, we have to address the *why*. It is true that each congregation has its own needs, so decisions which are essentially pastoral have to be made. Some honest questioning may reveal that the "new" hymn that we're just itching to use isn't the best thing for a particular Sunday in a particular place in the service in a particular parish.

But let's assume we have answered all the questions and still come up with a resounding "Yes, it's time to learn that one!" Here are some thoughts on how new music for worship can be introduced.

Congregations which regularly worship together usually require a period of time to assimilate worship habits. This includes changes in music or worship postures (e.g., standing for the prayers of the people) or changes in the order of service (e.g., introduction of a meditative silence after the lessons or the elimination of the Doxology at the offertory). Changes in worship habits don't happen suddenly. Hearing a hymn more than once a year is necessary.

A new hymn might be heard first as a choir anthem. This is often especially effective when introduced by children's voices—choral or solo. When the children like it and take it home to their families, there will already be a support group out there! Within the next few weeks the same hymn could reappear in a different guise, perhaps as music during the communion, with the choir singing the first stanzas alone and the congregation joining in on the last. (A notation in the bulletin stating the intention is a must!) Then in a few weeks, it could be scheduled as a congregational hymn, but probably not sung in procession. One more suggestion: congregations can become suspicious or downright hostile when a new hymn is used *too* often. It may be best to schedule this or other sequences with a space of a Sunday or so between. Then, it enters the congregation's consciousness without becoming boring.

The "hymn-of-the-month" is popular in some places. This technique can be effective, but watch for that glazed-over look that congregations can get when they're bored!

Some congregations respond very favorably to the "gathering-time rehearsal," perhaps instead of an opening voluntary. This lends an air of informality to the service, and again, pastoral considerations need to be made. In any case, the "rehearsal" should be dignified and brief, and should proceed smoothly and directly into the start of the service. Hint: if the parish musician is leading the rehearsal, it might be a good idea to allow that person to invite the congregation into worship by offering a brief prayer, or simply saying something like, "Please stand and join with me in God's praise as we sing hymn such-and-such." It's often a revelation to a congregation to hear the musician lead worship using the *spoken* voice.

One excellent teaching opportunity can be the "family choir." Some parishes have discovered that many parishioners would welcome an opportunity to sing in the choir but don't wish to make the required commitment. The intergenerational choir scheme could be the answer. Once-a-month rehearsals (following the Sunday service?) with a performance scheduled for the following Sunday may be just the thing. Throw in a pot-luck brunch after the rehearsal, and you may have a crowd on your hands! This group could also be the answer for the summer months when choirs tend to disappear.

The trick is to use "new" hymnal offerings as anthems which can then become congregational hymns when the group returns to the pew. Having a core of singers in the pews already in-the-know helps everyone. There is an added advantage if the family choir is truly "intergenerational." Peer pressure works! (Watch out, though; you might find that the family choir becomes a training choir for other ensembles, and you may have trouble maintaining it as members are drawn into these other groups!)

Church suppers are your golden opportunity! The benefits of the good old-fashioned "hymn sing" have been known to gatherings of the faithful for many years. Why not introduce one or two very carefully chosen "new" hymns in the midst of the "old chestnuts"? This is also a superb time to include some new service music. Perhaps the evening could begin with a few favorites, then introduce a new hymn which leads into the blessing for the meal. After dinner, sing some more hymns, old and new, and include one portion of new service music. The astute leader might also take the opportunity to teach the congregation some things about vocal production, singing style (not every hymn should be belted out, full-voice, after all), the history of hymnody, stories of composers, text writers, etc. And don't forget to end the evening with familiar music and prayer.

Doing this a few times each year can cover a lot of ground and become a much-loved event in the life of the parish.

Teaching congregations a new service music setting can provide more than a few headaches! Most of the suggestions made above for hymns will apply, especially of the congregational rehearsal, the family choir, and the church supper hymn sing. Remember, too, that congregations assimilate new materials over a period of time, so infrequent changing of service music settings usually works best. One possible goal could be "seasonal" settings, a new one added each year, building the full repertoire.

One of the best guides for the specifics of how to teach new music is found in the small booklet *Hymnal Studies Three: Teaching Music in the Small Church*, by Marilyn Keiser.[36] In this short document arising out of her work as music consultant for the Diocese of Western North Carolina in the 1970s, Dr. Keiser has provided a most comprehensive and logical guide for the teaching of music in congregations. Because this volume appeared in 1983 (before *The Hymnal 1982* was generally available), some of the references seem outdated, but the pedagogical suggestions are outstanding. This slim book should be in every Episcopal choir director's bookcase!

Finally, a word of caution: unless your congregation is particularly musically astute, don't introduce a lot of new worship material, hymns, or service music all at once or over a very short period of time.

In the opening pages of *Hymnal Studies Three: Teaching Music in the Small Church*, Marilyn Keiser quotes from Erik Routley, stating that "Art, being one of the manifestations of the Holy Spirit's work in the world, is a dimension of life—every man is an artist, a self-giver, a self-revealer, if he is allowed to be."[37]

Some of the themes of her book are then listed:

- We are all artists.
- For each worshiping community there is "a music."
- Simple sounds are often the most effective ones.
- Music is for people.[38]

To that I add that, because it is in the song of faith that we most *feel* the faith, we must enable each congregation to sing "its song"—the one that it already knows "by heart." With care, those "new songs" which have been carefully chosen, taught, and "caught" today will become the "old chestnuts" of tomorrow!

---

[36]Marilyn Keiser, *Hymnal Studies Three: Teaching Music in the Small Church*" (New York: The Church Hymnal Corporation, 1983).

[37]Erik Routley, *Words, Music, and the Church* (Nashville: Abington Press, 1968), p. 217.

[38]Keiser, Op, cit., p. 7.

How to Recruit Children and Adults for the Choir

by Judith Dodge

Churches large and small often will have years of great choral ministries then lean years of very poor choir participation. There are some parishes with no music tradition at all—and a hesitation to develop one—and parishes that have always had fine music. This can be attributed to many things: the music leadership, clergy leadership and support, interest in music in the community, quality of music in the public and private schools, the acoustics in the church, the choice of organ in the church, and the educational interests in the parish. All of these influences and many others not named will affect the development of choirs in a parish. What does *not* make a great difference is the *size* of the parish; large or small, good choirs can be developed for good worship in a church, enhancing that worship for all of the participants.

Years ago when I was developing a multiple choir program in an urban parish in one of our large cities, I was asked how I recruited people for the choirs. My immediate answer, without even thinking was, "One person at a time." I would still give that answer. A choir is built *one person at a time*.

Knowing and understanding the local situation is the key to the approach for recruiting choir singers, and, because each situation is different, one cannot imitate another's successes. The first decision to be made is what kind of choir(s) to have: An all adult choir? A "mixed" choir of adults and children (a model used very successfully in some English parishes and a few American churches)? A choir just for boys? Just for girls? Just for children? Just for teens? A choir of men and boys? Men, boys, and girls? A women's choir? The next question must be the purposes of the choir. Will it sing for only one service on a Sunday morning? Is that service always a eucharist? Is there morning prayer? Is there evensong? Will there be special services such as lessons and carols? Ash Wednesday? Easter Vigil? What demands will there be on the singers?

Once the needs of the parish worship traditions and the kind of choir(s) best suited for the traditions have been determined, goals can be set: establishing rehearsal schedules and a singing schedule for services. People who are to be recruited must know what they are committing to. And from the beginning, those expectations must be established. It is also suggested that, from the start, choristers be expected to attend weekly rehearsal schedules and sing weekly services. This is true of children as well, except for the very young. The more frequently choirs sing, the better they get at what they do, and better choirs draw more people to sing in them.

Publicity is an all-important tool for choir recruitment; people need to know that a choir is starting, or growing, or that it encourages additional membership. All the obvious public relations gimmicks can and should be used, including posters in the church, items in the newsletter or bulletin, and articles in the local newspaper. Personal appeals can also be made at church meetings and functions, and in Sunday school classes, as long as the leaders of these other church groups do not see the choirs as competing for the time of their people. (Must we really hold Sunday warm-up rehearsals during the adult Sunday forum hour, or take children out of Sunday school for rehearsals?)

The repertory a choir sings often determines its membership. The Episcopal church has a fine tradition of outstanding music and is known throughout the country for its good liturgical music and fine choirs. Quality is a key element in determining that reputation: good music done well. This music does not have to be of a certain style or tradition or period. It does not have to be difficult or challenging. But to reiterate, it must be of high quality and done well, and—for a greater success in worship—it must fit the liturgy, the texts, the ideas. Music must be selected with care and taught with care. If these things are considered and carried out, the mystery and beauty of the worship will work to enhance the singing. And one by one, people will come to ask about membership in the choir.

Special concerts or music dramas or musicals outside of the church service schedule will often draw new members from those people interested in being a part of something successful, and those interested in being a part of something that has quality and looks like fun. There are simple, effective, and often short musicals that can be produced with very simple means that serve to draw new people to the music program.

Recruiting can be accomplished very effectively by the non-musical members of the parish as well as the regular members of the choir. Whenever church friends show appreciation to the choir director for the music, ask those friends to serve as "spies" and help spot potential choir members, welcoming them and suggesting they join the choir. I have a church friend who enthusiastically supports the music in our worship by greeting newcomers with the line, "Hello and welcome! Are you an alto or soprano (or tenor or bass)?"

Choir trips, exchanges with other church choirs, or joint programs with other churches—as well as in-house workshops for choral development and participation in summer choir training sessions—also serve to enhance choir recruitment. If potential singers know that they will continue to receive training and continue to develop and learn about music and singing, their reasons to join will be increased. This is especially true of parents who want their children to sing. Years ago, a parent approached me explaining very apologetically that he wanted his son to be in the choir, but the son couldn't sing. My response was that being unable to sing was exactly why the boy *should* be in the choir—so that he could learn to sing. The parent was right; the boy *couldn't* sing! But as a fourth grader, he joined the choir, and by the eighth grade—when his voice changed—he was one of my finest choristers! Since then, he has gone on to one of the best music schools in the country as a keyboard player, and he performs jazz brilliantly. Choirs help singers find their voices.

Many large churches are finding that small groups provide ways for individuals to find fellowship and involvement in an otherwise anonymous institution. Even in small churches, the choirs provide that "small group" intimacy that is so successful. Fellowship within a choir is an invaluable tool for recruitment, especially if the present members of the choir are open and responsive to having an "empty chair" always available for a new member of the group. Choir parties, social gatherings of choir family members (such as picnics or other outings) are wonderful opportunities for people to get to know each other, and are of critical importance in choir recruitment. Do your singers have fun?

Recruitment must be inclusive if the intent is to build a choir. The term "audition" is a frightening prospect for almost all singers. More useful, once a choir is established, is to have "voice hearings" in order to hear and evaluate individual choristers for use in assigning parts, finding vocal problems, and having an opportunity to do a bit of vocal coaching. This is a good thing to do once a year or every other year in order to keep track of the abilities in the choir. But unless you are prepared to have a truly "professional" choir, auditioning has but a very tiny place in the overall scheme of choir recruitment.

Is the worship space "choir-friendly"? An unfriendly space may actually keep people out of the choir. What does the choir sound like in the acoustic of the church? Is it a "live" space or a "dry" space? Does the organ overwhelm the singing? If piano accompanies the choir, is it a good instrument, and is it kept in tune? Does the choir sit in a place that is comfortable, with good lighting, where it can hear well and be heard? Is the choir physically a part of the worship? These are key questions for potential singers, although they themselves may not know this. Many good singers would rather sit in the congregation to worship than be stuck behind pillars or in corners where the sermon from a fine preacher becomes a non-event. Are your singers able to worship?

The choir director is also a key music educator in the community. Hence, the personality of the choir director is as important in the recruitment process as the skills that director brings to the position. Being welcoming, being approachable, being positive, and—especially—being a "team player" in the total worship ministry of the church is very important. In addition, effective use of rehearsal time is also a recruiting tool. Do prospective members know that their time will not be wasted time? Whether it's a cathedral choir or a small parish choir, any choir director who stands in front of a group of singers must be vigilant about making sure that their time spent together is being used well for everyone.

Some choir directors may want access to ongoing training. There are wonderful church musician summer institutes and conferences that help build and develop the skills of a music educator. Many are conducted at local colleges and universities while others are sponsored by seminaries and dioceses. Some of the most outstanding summer programs are planned and directed by: the Royal School of Church Music in American (call (216) 836-1511 for information); Westminster Choir College in Princeton, New Jersey; the Mississippi Conference on Liturgy and Music (based at St. Philip's in Jackson), the Evergreen Conference in Colorado (contact St. John's Cathedral in Denver); and the Sewanee Conference (contact the School of Theology at the University of the South in Sewanee, Tennessee) to name a few. These programs are valuable for both experienced and inexperienced choir directors, and, yes, will answer questions about choir recruiting.

To summarize, here is a list of basic important considerations as one begins to recruit members for choirs:

- Determine the number of choirs to have and their make-up.
- Decide what are the purposes and goals of the choir(s).
- Plan the choir schedule of rehearsals and services.
- Plan publicity, both in-house and in the community.
- Determine and develop the repertory for the choir, taking into consideration the liturgy, the worship traditions of the parish, the community music skills, and the time of preparation. Aim for high quality.
- Plan to have a special concert or program in addition to the regular service schedule.
- Use non-musical members of the congregation to assist in recruiting.
- Plan a program of skill development for all the singers. Have teaching be a major part of the program. Don't waste people's time.
- Understand that the choir is a "small group" within the larger parish which means it must be inclusive. Make the choir a welcoming place for people.
- Plan social events for the choir.
- Develop a worship space that is choir-friendly. Can your singers also worship when they sing in the choir?

- Understand that the key to a fine choir is the director. A good director is a good musician and a good educator. Have teaching be a major part of the program.

And finally, it is well to remember that choristers are recruited one at a time; and choristers must be recruited all the time.

For Further Reading

(Listed by article in order of appearance.)

Worship and the Ministry of the Baptized

The Baptizing Community, A. Theodore Eastman, Morehouse Publishing Company, Harrisburg, PA, 1991.

Baptism and Ministry, Liturgical Studies I, The Church Hymnal Corporation, New York, 1994.

Remember Who You Are; Baptism, a Model for Christian Life, William H. Willimon, The Upper Room, Nashville, TN, 1980.

Baptismal Moments, Baptismal Meanings, Daniel B. Stevik, The Church Hymnal Corporation, New York, 1987.

The Catechumenal Process, The Church Hymnal Corporation, New York, 1990.

The Shape of Baptism, Aidan Kavanaugh, Pueblo Publishing Company, New York, 1978.

Who's in Charge Here?

The Ceremonies of the Eucharist, Howard E. Galley, Cowley Publications, Cambridge, MA, 1989.

Deacons in the Liturgy, Ormonde Plater, Morehouse Publishing Company, Harrisburg, PA, 1992.

The Development of Style in Worship

Articles and books cited here consider components of liturgical style historically. Many, but not all, of them consider the particulars of liturgical style culturally as well. These resources are relatively brief "start-up" readings. Should you wish to pursue the issues more fully, you will find additional sources cited in the articles.

Handbooks and Dictionaries

The following three references are general, up-to-date collections of articles on liturgical topics; these are followed by specific articles cited from these general collections and organized by category.

The New Dictionary of Sacramental Worship, Peter E. Fink, ed., Michael Glazier/ Liturgical Press, Collegeville, MN, 1990.

Despite its title, the scope of this work covers all forms of the liturgy, not just the sacraments. It is Roman Catholic in origin but ecumenical in scope.

The New Westminster Dictionary of Liturgy and Worship, J. G. Davies, ed., Westminster, Philadelphia, 1986.

This is a substantial revision of a work first published in 1972. It includes brief, explanatory entries as well as more substantial essays.

The Study of the Liturgy, revised edition, Cheslyn Jones, Geoffrey Wainwright, Edward Yarnold, and Paul Bradshaw, eds., Oxford University Press, New York, 1992.

This is a partial revision of a work first published in 1978. The primary focus of the work is on initiation, the eucharist, ordination, and the office, but matters related to style are treated in Part One, "Theology and Rite," and Part Two, Section VII, "The Setting of the Liturgy."

Vesture

The following articles place issues of vesture in both historical and contemporary contexts.

"Vestments, Liturgical," John D. Lawrence, in Fink, *Dictionary*.

"Vestments," W. Jardine Grisbrooke, in Jones et al., *Study of the Liturgy*.

"Vestments," Gilbert Cope, in Davies, *New Dictionary*.

Ceremonial

"Gestures," Gilbert Cope, and "Movements in Worship," J. G. Davies, in Davies, *New Dictionary*.

"Ritual," Mark Searle, and "Ceremonial," Hugh Wybrew, in Jones, *Study of the Liturgy*.

"Gesture and Movement in the Liturgy," Thomas A. Korsnicki, and "Gestures, Liturgical," Robert Vereecke, in Fink, *Dictionary*.

Strong, Loving, and Wise: Presiding in the Liturgy, Robert W. Hovda, Liturgical Conference, Washington, DC, 1977.

This is a guide in the Roman Catholic tradition for those who preside at the eucharist. This resource treats ceremonial issues with a strong sensitivity. There is much wisdom to be gleaned from those in other traditions!

Prayer Book Rubrics Expanded, Byron D. Stuhlman, The Church Hymnal Corporation, New York, 1987.

The author of "The Development of Style in Worship" has written a guide to planning and leading worship which expands upon many of the issues addressed in his article.

The Architectural Setting

"Architecture, Liturgical," Mary M. Schaefer, in Fink, *New Dictionary*.

"The Architectural Setting of the Liturgy," Peter G. Cobb, in Jones, *Study of the Liturgy*.
"Architectural Setting," J. G. Davies, and "Architectural Setting (Modern) and the Liturgical Movement," F. Debuyst, in Davies, *New Dictionary*.
"Architectural Implications of the Book of Common Prayer," Marion J. Hatchett, in *Occasional Papers of the Standing Liturgical Commission: Collection Number One*, The Church Hymnal Corporation, New York, 1987.

Liturgy and Culture

"Culture, Liturgy," M. Francis Mannion, and "Inculturation of the Liturgy," Peter Schineller, in Fink, *Dictionary*.
"Indigenization," John G. Englan, in Davies, *New Dictionary*.

With What Words Shall We Pray?

Naming the Mystery: How Our Words Shape Prayer and Belief, James E. Griffiss, Cowley Publications, Cambridge, MA, 1990.
A work by a noted Episcopal theologian which addresses the questions of the use of feminine language and female images of God.
How Shall We Pray, Liturgical Studies Two, Ruth A. Meyers, ed., The Church Hymnal Corporation, New York, 1994.
A collection of papers presented in a theological consultation on Supplemental Liturgical Materials along with discussion and response.
Christ in Sacred Speech: The Meaning of Liturgical Language, Gail Ramshaw-Schmidt, Fortress Press, Philadelphia, 1986.
An exploration of the role and use of liturgical language by a Lutheran liturgical scholar.
Searching for Language, Gail Ramshaw, The Pastoral Press, Washington, DC, 1988.
A collection of articles reflecting upon theological language in the context of worship.
The Revised Common Lectionary, Abingdon Press, Nashville, TN, 1992.

Preaching and Praying the Lectionary

In Dialogue With Scripture: An Episcopal Guide to Studying the Bible, Linda Grenz, ed., The Episcopal Church Center, New York, 1993.
The Inviting Word, Sidney D. Fowler, ed., United Church Press, Cleveland, OH.
Complete curriculum developed by the United Church of Christ. Includes three volumes of lection-based commentaries and age-level leader and learner guides.

Liturgical Space and the Proclamation of the Gospel

A Church for Common Prayer, The Church Building Fund, New York, 1994.

An excellent, concise overview of the main considerations to be kept in mind when contemplating changes to an existing building or designing a new one. As close as the Episcopal Church gets to an official statement on church architecture.

Where We Worship, Walter C. Huffman and Anita Stauffer, Augsburg Publishing, Minneapolis, MN, 1987.

An excellent study book and leader's guide prepared by the Evangelical Lutheran Church in America (E.L.C.A.). The two books present a summary of the history of Christian architecture and the alternatives possible today.

Environment and Art in Catholic Worship, The National Conference of Catholic Bishops.

The official American Roman Catholic statement on church art and architecture, it stresses the principles of quality and appropriateness in the design and furnishing of churches.

Beyond the Text: A Holistic Approach to Liturgy, Lawrence A. Hoffman, Indiana University Press, Bloomington, IN, 1989.

See especially, Chapter 7, "The Numinous, a Problem of Recognition." Hoffman stresses the need for a sacred environment that goes beyond the nineteenth-century sense of the sacred.

Jesus Wants to Dance!—In Church—With Us!!!

Congregational Dancing in Christian Worship, Doug Adams, The Sharing Company, Austin, TX, 1971.

Dance as Religious Studies, Doug Adams and Diane Apostolos-Cappadona, eds., Crossroad Publishing, New York, 1990.

Liturgical Dance: An Historical, Theological and Practical Handbook, J. G. Davies, S.C.M. Press, Ltd., London, 1984.

The Dancing Church (videotape), Thomas Kane, Paulist Press, Mahwah, NJ, 1992.

Greek Dances and How to Do Them (You Don't Have to be Greek), Ted Petrides, Peters International, New York.

Book with records or cassette tapes.

How to Celebrate the Triduum

Celebrating Redemption, Associated Parishes, Fort Worth, TX.

A brochure from Associated Parishes about the liturgies of Lent, Holy Week, and Easter. Inexpensive, so order several copies.

The Triduum Sourcebook, Liturgy Training Publications, Chicago.
A rich collection of homilies, prayers, liturgical texts for the liturgies of the Triduum.

The Prayer Book Office, Howard E. Galley, ed., The Church Hymnal Corporation, New York, 1994.
This is a reissue of the familiar resource formerly published by Seabury Press.

The Hymnal 1982: Service Music, Accompaniment Edition Volume 1, The Church Hymnal Corporation, New York.
Music for the Triduum. See S68–S70 and S344–S352.

Gradual Psalms, Church Hymnal Series VI, Parts I, II, III, The Church Hymnal Corporation, New York, 1980–82.
More music for the Triduum.

Additional Resources

A Prayer Book for the 21st Century, Liturgical Studies 3, Ruth A. Meyers, ed., The Church Hymnal Corporation, New York, 1996.
Essays on the principal issues that will need to be addressed in a future version of the Book of Common Prayer.

Shaped by Images, William Seth Adams, The Church Hymnal Corporation, New York, 1995.
An important book for liturgical planners. The author addresses the subject of the formation of liturgical ministry and ministers. The reader is then encouraged to translate this understanding into liturgical practice.

About the Authors

J. Fletcher Lowe, Jr. is a baptized Christian who, in his ministry as an ordained person, has served communities of the baptized in South Carolina, Virginia, and Delaware. He was the organizer and first chair of the Liturgical Commissions in Southwestern Virginia (1965–67) and Virginia (1967–71), chaired the Episcopal Church's National Hunger Committee (1974–82), served on the Board of the Presiding Bishop's Fund for World Relief (1987–92), and is an honorary canon of St. Peter's Cathedral in the Diocese of Bukdei, Uganda. He lives in Richmond, Virginia, and is currently involved in a ministry to the world's children through The Christian Children's Fund.

Ormonde Plater is a deacon at Grace Church in New Orleans, where he helps coordinate an interparochial ministry in hospitals. A member of the Council of Associated Parishes, he is author of *Many Servants* (1991) and *Deacons in the Liturgy* (1992) and co-author of *Cajun Dancing* (1993). He edits the newsletter *Diakoneo* for the North American Association for the Diaconate.

Byron D. Stuhlman, ordained priest in 1966, is canonically resident in the Diocese of Connecticut, where he served as a parish priest for more than twenty years and as chair of the Diocesan Liturgical Commission for ten years. He then undertook graduate studies at Duke University and was granted a doctorate in 1991 for a dissertation on the liturgical theology of Alexander Schmemann. For two years, he taught as a visiting professor at Hamilton College and now does supply work in the Diocese of Central New York. He served a term as president of the Association of Diocesan Liturgy and Music Commissions and was the founder and first editor of its newsletter. He is the author of three books published by the Church Hymnal Corporation and has edited copy for the second volume of *The Hymnal 1982 Companion*. He is currently preparing two other books for publication.

Thomas McCart is Rector of St. Mark's, Upland, California, and former Canon Precentor of Christ Church Cathedral, Indianapolis. A musician and a priest, McCart has served in a variety of parishes and cathedrals and is actively involved in the Association of Anglican Musicians and the Association of Diocesan Liturgy and Music Commissions. He received his doctorate in Church History from Vanderbilt University in 1994. He is a frequent speaker on hymns and the development of hymnody, and his first book on the subject was published by Drew University in 1995.

Jean Campbell is a member of the Order of St. Helena, a monastic community in the Episcopal Church. She was ordained priest in 1990. She was a member of the initial sub-committee on supplemental texts and from 1988–94 served as vice chair of the Standing Liturgical Commission and chair of the sub-committee on supplemental texts. A member of the North American Academy of Liturgy, the Association of Diocesan Liturgy and Music Commissions, the Council of Associated Parishes, and the Liturgy Commission of the Diocese of New York, she is a leader of workshops and conferences in the fields of liturgical spirituality and catechesis.

Charles N. Fulton III has been President of the Episcopal Church Building Fund since 1990, having first served as Vice President. As a priest, he served parishes in Tennessee for nearly twenty years. He has had liturgical and architectural experience on the local, diocesan, and national levels.

J. M. C. Oliver is the Canon Missioner for the Diocese of New Jersey and an artist. While a doctoral student in worship and the arts at the Graduate Theological Union in Berkeley, California, he founded Living Ritual, a company specializing in liturgical consultation and design.

Ralph Carskadden is Rector of St. Clement's, Seattle. He holds degrees in music, theology, and the fine arts. He has served parishes in Tacoma, Washington, and in Grosse Pointe and Detroit, Michigan, and was Rector from 1979–86 of All Souls', San Diego. He serves as a liturgical arts consultant and continues work in ceramics in his studio in Seattle.

Marilyn L. Haskel was Director of Parish Music at St. Paul's in Walnut Creek, California, until 1995 when she became Marketing Director for the Church Hymnal Corporation. She is chair of the Standing Commission on Church Music; music editor for "OPEN," the newsletter of Associated Parishes; former president and newsletter editor of the Association of Diocesan Liturgy and Music Commissions; and a member of the Association of Anglican Musicians. She is also a frequent workshop leader in the area of music and liturgy and conductor of choral events for children's music ministry.

Joseph Russell is the retired Canon to the Ordinary for Education and Program for the Diocese of Ohio. He has produced curriculum materials for several church-related organizations and, most recently, was a writer for the United Church of Christ's new lectionary-based curriculum. In 1995, he became an associate of Leader Resources, a consortium of church educators recently formed to serve dioceses and congregations of the church.

Richard Fabian is a founding Rector of St. Gregory Nyssen Episcopal Church, San Francisco, a member of Societas Liturgica, the North American Academy of Liturgy, and the International Anglican Liturgical Consultation. He lectures at the California

School for Deacons, and chairs the Diocese of California Liturgy and Music Commission. Fr. Fabian wrote music for *The Hymnal 1982* and *Congregational Music for Eucharist (Church Hymnal Series V)*. He has written articles on alternative worship in the liturgical tradition for *The Complete Library of Christian Worship*. Formerly Episcopal Chaplain at Yale University, he studied at Yale, Cambridge, the College of the Resurrection (Mirfield, England), and the General Theological Seminary. His most sacred hobbies are swimming, snowboarding, and collecting Chinese art.

Ernesto Medina is the Missioner for Christian Education in the Diocese of Los Angeles. He is a native Californian, currently living in San Gabriel with his wife, Susan, and two children, Eric and Elizabeth. He served four years as chair of the Diocesan Commission for Liturgy and Church Music in Los Angeles and is currently the President-elect of the Association of Diocesan Liturgy and Music Commissions. As an active participant in the "Treasure Kids! Project," Ernie works for the full inclusion of children in the total life of the church.

Clayton L. Morris is Liturgical Officer for the Episcopal Church. A priest and church musician, he has worked variously as curate, rector, organist-choirmaster, and director of liturgy and music in congregations in the Diocese of California. In his role as Liturgical Officer, he coordinates the work of the Standing Liturgical Commission and Standing Commission on Church Music, assists the Presiding Bishop as liturgical consultant, and serves as liaison to the variety of organizations within the Episcopal Church which concern themselves with liturgy and music.

Joseph Robinson is Dean of St. Andrew's Cathedral in Jackson, Mississippi, where he lives with his wife, Diane, and their two children. He was the former Canon Precentor at St. John's Episcopal Cathedral in Denver. His hobbies include many types of music, iconography, and downhill skiing.

Gretchen Wolff Pritchard is well known as a speaker and clinician in Christian education, liturgy, and children's spirituality. She is the creator of *The Sunday Paper* materials for children. She works in Christian education at St. Paul's Church in New Haven, Connecticut.

Michael Merriman is priest-in-charge of The Church of Gethsemane in Minneapolis. He has served on the Standing Liturgical Commission and was president of the Association of Diocesan Liturgy and Music Commissions. Prior to his position as Precentor at Grace Cathedral, San Francisco, he served as rector of parishes in Texas. He edited and contributed to *The Baptismal Mystery and the Catechumenate* and publishes a series of liturgical commentaries called *The People's Work*.

Mark T. Engelhardt is Organist and Director of Music for the Cathedral Church of St. Paul in Boston and is music consultant for the Diocese of Massachusetts. Prior to his Boston appointment in 1989, he served churches in New York, Kansas City, Mississippi, and Louisiana. As a church music professional, he has held positions of leadership at the local, diocesan, and national levels of the Episcopal Church. He is popular as the music director for conferences, choral festivals, and choir camps.

Judith Dodge is Director of Music/Organist at St. Columba's Episcopal Church in Washington, D.C., a position she held from 1972 to 1983 and to which she returned in 1993. Her forte is choir-building which she has done in Washington, D.C., Kalamazoo, Michigan, and Tucson, Arizona. Her music degrees are from the University of Colorado and San Francisco State University. In addition to being a church musician, she has taught music in public schools, was Assistant Director of the San Francisco Boys' Chorus, served on the Artistic Advisory Board of the Gilmore International Keyboard Festival, directed choral music at Kalamazoo College, and was Director of the Kalamazoo Bach Festival. She has served as the President of the Association of Anglican Musicians.